1945

# Weep Not for Me
# Dear Mother

# Weep Not for Me Dear Mother

Elizabeth Whitley Roberson

Drawings by
Stephen McCall

PELICAN PUBLISHING COMPANY
Gretna 1998

First Pelican edition, January 1996
Second printing, April 1998
First hardcover edition, April 1998

---

*The word "Pelican" and the depiction of a pelican are
trademarks of Pelican Publishing Company, Inc., and are
registered in the U.S. Patent and Trademark Office.*

---

**Library of Congress Cataloging-in-Publication Data**

Roberson, Elizabeth Whitley.
    Weep not for me, dear mother / Elizabeth Whitley Roberson ;
drawings by Stephen McCall. — 1st Pelican ed.
      p.   cm.
    Includes index.
    ISBN 1-56554-389-0 (hc : alk. paper) — ISBN 1-56554-390-4 (pbk. : alk. paper)
    1. Landers, Eli Pinson—Correspondence. 2. United States—History—Civil War, 1861-
1865—Personal narratives, Confederate. 3. Confederate States of America. Army. Georgia
Infantry Regiment, 16th—Biography. 4. Georgia—History—Civil War, 1861-1865—Personal
narratives. 5. Soldiers—Georgia—Gwinnett County—Correspondence. 6. Gwinnett County
(Ga.)—Biography. I. Title
E503.5 16th.R63 1996
973.7'458—dc20
                                         95-26298
                                              CIP

Manufactured in the United States of America

Published by Pelican Publishing Company, Inc.
P.O. Box 3110, Gretna, Louisiana 70054-3110

This book is dedicated to the men of the 5th Mo/9th Ga. Regiment of re-enactors of Lilburn, Georgia, whose generosity of both time and money made possible the fulfilment of the final requests of Eli Pinson Landers, who died in defense of his beloved state of Georgia; and to the descendents of Eli Landers who still today personify those values for which Eli fought and died; and to my children, who share my love of our Southern heritage. Finally, I wish to dedicate this book to my friend Donald Torrence, Sr., without whose help it would not have been possible.

# Contents

*PREFACE*

THE DAY I CAME into the possession of a bundle of letters written by Eli Pinson Landers to his mother, Susan Landers, little did I realize what was in store for me. For finding out who Eli Landers was, has led me on a veritable treasure hunt through six states, from the Civil War battlegrounds in Pennsylvania, Maryland and Virginia to Eli's beloved Gwinnett County homeplace in the hill country of North Georgia.

It was through the most unlikely and fortuitous combination of coincidence and sheer luck that the letters reached me at all. In truth, I cannot help feeling that they were somehow meant to fall into my hands—into the hands of an historian who could understand and appreciate them and who would write about them.

How did the Eli Landers' correspondence reach me? The story begins in the mid-1960's, in Atlanta, Georgia. I was told that "a woman"-someone whose name I have never been able to learn—noticed a sheaf of stained, yellowed letters in a pile of trash on a street in Atlanta. The letters interested her. She picked one of the letters up and was immediately struck by the fine penmanship so typical of other eras. This letter was undoubtedly very old, she knew. Then she saw the date at the top of it and realized that it had been written during the time of the Civil War. She carefully gathered all of them up and took them home with her.

Once home, Eli Pinson's rescuer no doubt read through the correspondence and realized its intrinsic interest. Yet she did not know quite what to do with these fragile documents in which a young voice spoke so clearly and poignantly of a time long past. Later on, she moved to Raleigh,North Carolina and carried the letters with her. There in Raleigh, she became acquainted with young Ricky Mobley, the son of a neighbor and a boy whom she knew to be interested in history and things historical. She decided to give the letters to him since he would, she felt, appreciate and understand them.

A few years later, the Mobleys moved back to their home in Williamston, North Carolina, bringing the letters with them. They packed them away in a closet where they stayed for several more years. One day in the fall of 1989, Ricky's mother, Nellie, knowing of my interest in the Civil War, called me and asked if I would like to see the letters.

I went to get them immediately, and much to my surprise, found not just a small bundle of letters, as I had expected, but a bag full, numbering about one hundred in all. I realized very quickly that just reading the letters in a random order was quite confusing, so I began sorting them into chronological order.

The first letter, dated August 11,1861 was written on the morning Eli left home after he had enlisted in Howell Cobb's regiment, the Flint Hill Grays. After completing my task, I found that the letters abruptly ended in 1863.

The more I read the letters, the more I realized that I must find out everything I could about their author-who he was, what he was like, who his family was, and most importantly, why the letters stopped so suddenly in 1863.

I first wrote to the National Archives in Washington,DC requesting any information they could give me about Eli Pinson Landers. When they responded, they said that they had not only his service record, but his pension records as well. From that bit of information, I surmised that if he had applied for a pension, he must have survived the war. The day the records arrived, I could hardly wait to read them,but my joy was short-lived, however, when I realized that the Eli Landers' pension records were for another man by the same name. "My" Eli's service record indicated that he died just after the last letter was written.

My search for Eli Landers had only begun, however,

and my sights turned to Gwinnett County, Georgia, a place he mentioned so many times in his letters. I found a directory of newspapers in America and located the names of two papers published in that county, The Gwinnett *Daily News* and the Gwinnett *Home Weekly*. I wrote to the editors of both papers asking them to publish my letter requesting relatives of the Landers family to contact me. In about a week, I received a call from Evelyn Mays. When she said she was calling from Lilburn, Georgia, my heart sang, for I knew the connection had been made. In my preliminary research on Gwinnett County, I had found that Lilburn was the name given to the little community of Yellow River where Eli lived. Evelyn Mays told me that her great-grandmother, Elizabeth, had been Eli's sister and that she had information about the family that she would like to share with me if I would go down to Georgia.

In a few weeks, I was able to make the trip to Lilburn, where I met several members of the family and located the little log cabin that had been the home of Eli's mother, Susan McDaniel Landers. I also found the Sweetwater Church he mentioned so often in his letters, as well as the little graveyard where he was buried.

I shall never forget my feelings that day as I stood by the small, neglected headstone. It was so covered in green moss that the name Eli P. Landers was barely visible. I felt that this boy, who gave up so much fighting for a cause in which he believed so strongly, should have had a monument befitting his sacrifice. I remembered that in one of his last letters to his mother that he had asked that, if he should die, to have a tombstone engraved, not only with his name, but also with his dates of service to the Confederacy and a list of all the battles in which he had fought. Apparently, due to lack of money, his request had not been honored.

It is difficult to describe my feelings as I looked out on the green pastures behind Eli's grandmother's cabin remembering how he stated over and over again in his letters that his greatest wish was to come back and again roam those fields in Gwinnett County on his mare Kate, and to tend the little farm with his mother and sisters. Eli's request was such a simple one, but, sadly, one that could not be fulfilled. I came back to North

Carolina feeling somehow that I knew Eli a little better since I had actually seen his home and the fields he so lovingly described.

While I was in Lilburn, a reporter from the *Daily News* interviewed me. When the article was published, the story was picked up by the Associated Press, taking it into Alabama, Tennessee, and Florida. So, my next call came from Mary Landers Shelton in Jacksonville, Alabama, whose great grandfather had been Eli's half-brother, Humphrey Davis Landers. She invited me for a visit, so I headed south again. I spent several days there in North Alabama meeting more members of the Landers family and collecting photographs of the family and pictures of Eli's brother's old homeplace.

After making contact with the family, I set out to retrace Eli's path through the battle sites in Virginia. His first stop had been in Richmond, where he described to his mother all the things he saw there, among which were statues of George Washington and Henry Clay. I found the same statues, and as I stood looking up at the statue of Washington as Eli said, "standing on a stack of fine rock", I could just imagine how this young farm boy, away from home for the first time, must have felt as he looked up at the same massive piece of granite.

My next trip was to Fredericksburg and Chancellorsville where Eli lived and fought in the winter of 1862. I stood there "behind the stone wall", trying to picture that awful carnage that Eli described so vividly. I saw the "sunken road" and wondered how Eli must have felt seeing so many dead and dying soldiers there.

Later, I visited the Peninsula near Yorktown where Eli Landers' regiment met the Union army at the battles of Lee's Mill and Dam Number One. Even though a large housing project is now encroaching on the Lee's Mill site, there was enough of the earthenworks remaining when I visited the area to see the Confederates' position there. At the Dam I saw the same water-filled trenches in which the Georgia regiment had to stand for days on end without fire or shelter.

One last visit to Virginia took me to northern Virginia to find Crampton's Gap at South Mountain to see for myself what kind of terrain Eli's regiment had to cross. The drive from

Richmond took four hours in my car, while Eli describes thirteen days of hard marching to cover the same ground. It was very serene there on the snow covered slopes of South Mountain the day I visited the site. What a contrast with that day in the fall of 1862 when over two thirds of Eli's regiment was killed on those same slopes!

Before I could actually finish writing Eli's story, I felt that in order to make my research complete,I must visit the battlefield of Gettysburg. Though there were no letters describing the battle,there was in with the letters a small pencilled note describing the route he took in getting there. This then was the route I traveled as well. I knew that as a part of Wofford's Brigade, Eli's regiment participated in the second day's battle which was fought at the peach orchard, through the wheat field,to the forbidding rocks of the Devil's Den. That battle was fought on July 2nd, 1863. I visited the area on July 12th,1991 when the temperature was nearly one hundred degrees, so experiencing the terrible heat alone helped me better understand the hardships the troops must have endured there.

After collecting all the photographs and background material I could find on the Sixteenth Georgia Regiment, I began to write Eli's story,using his letters to give life to the abstract account of the events of the war.

Because the article in the Gwinnett paper quoted Eli's request for a tombstone, Jimmy Dodd, a member of the 5th Missouri/9th Georgia group of re-enactors there in Lilburn,called me and said that his regiment wanted to erect a new stone for Eli in keeping with the one he had requested in 1863. Jimmy had a double interest in the project, since he not only wanted to honor a Civil War soldier's request, but also to honor his own wife, Theresa, a descendant of Eli's brother James Landers. So, on September 23, 1990, one hundred and twenty seven years after his death, I had the honor of attending a special memorial service and dedication of the new tombstone for Eli Landers at the Sweetwater Church he loved so much. With the traditional twenty-one gun salute over his grave, Eli was finally given the honors he so richly deserved.

I thought surely nothing else in my search would be as thrilling as that ceremony, but a few weeks after I returned home, I received a photograph from a descendant of Eli's sister, Adaline, who said that it just might be of Eli, but he couldn't be positive about it. By using a clue I had picked up in one of Eli's letters to his mother, I was able to confirm that the photograph was indeed one of Eli Landers. Eli had written of an ambrotype he had had made for his mother after he arrived in Richmond, saying that he had written his name on his cartridge box. With the aid of a magnifying glass, I found his initials, EPL plainly visible, just as he had described them to his mother. How happy I was to finally see the person I had gotten to know so well through a bundle of old letters. The young face, the strong hands, the sensitive eyes all bespoke those qualities I had sensed in his letters. His devotion to his family, his history of hard work in the red clay fields of Georgia, his honesty and integrity, were all mirrored in his photograph, and he almost seemed to reach out to me from its frame to say, "Thank you for telling my story."

The Civil War was the most devastating war ever fought by Americans-certainly to the American land itself. It resulted in the loss of over a half million of America's young men, the effects of which would be felt for many years after it was over.

It is always amazing to read of the odds against which the Confederate soldiers fought. They were outnumbered in every battle, but still marched onto the battlefield confident of victory. They faced an enemy who had superior weapons and unlimited supplies of food and equipment. They received less pay than the Union soldier and the money they did receive had less value. They also had to worry about their homes and families, since the most of the fighting took place on southern soil. They endured dust in the summer and mud in the winter. Some accounts of the war tell of mud so deep that it would completely submerge horses and mules. Sometimes during a rainy season, a soldier would literally have to pull his fellow soldiers from mudholes in the roads. They were out in all kinds of weather and would sometimes march for many miles in the rain, living for weeks on end in wet clothes, sleeping under soggy blankets, and eating cold food.

Shortages of food were common and sometimes troops would go two or three days with nothing to eat. When the

Confederate government weakened to the point that it could not furnish food, the men had to forage for what they got. Some were even reduced to eating the corn that was meant for the horses.

Most of the men had no clear idea as to what they were fighting for. They fought out of a strong sense of honor, for what they called "Southern rights" and ultimately for the defense of their homeland. There were some, in the beginning, who thought of the war simply as an exciting adventure that would be over in a matter of days.

What really kept these young men going in the face of the terrible deprivations and hardships that befell them as the war dragged on? We are unlikely to find the answer to this question in any history book. More likely, we will discover it in personal letters the soldiers wrote to their families back home, for it is in those letters that they expressed their hopes, fears, and sorrows.

Eli Pinson Landers of the Sixteenth Georgia Regiment of volunteers was one such individual. He poured out his most innermost feelings in letters to his mother, Susan, who lived in the little rural community of Yellow River (now Lilburn) in Gwinnett County, Georgia.

As I read Eli Landers' letters it was as if I had opened a window of the Landers home, through which I could look in at them, yet not be seen. I began experiencing their joys, their sorrows, their disappointments. My perspective on the war changed. Here I saw a man willing to die for the cause, as he saw it, of freedom of choice and independence. I found that slavery, in this case, at least, was not the driving force that sent a young Southern boy out to fight other Americans. Eli Landers' family had no slaves to help tend their farm, but worked the land themselves, raising small acreages of corn, cotton, and wheat. In fact, Eli worried constantly about his mother, who was left at home with his sisters, who now had to plow the fields and harvest the crops without the help of a man.

Eli was only nineteen years old when the war began, and with the enthusiasm of a teenager, entered the conflict with great optimism and a belief in an early victory. As the casualties mounted, however, this excitement waned considerably. Because of the horrors he had witnessed, when he died at the age of twenty one, he had become one who was old beyond his years.

The letters reveal other information that was painful to read at times, such as Eli's reaction to the death of his little nephew William Henry, whom he loved so dearly. In another letter, Eli showed great concern about his sister Adaline having been caught for stealing, something that in gentler times she would have never done. I experienced the anguish his mother and sister must have felt as they battled against time, trying to get to the Atlanta railroad station to see Eli when he came in from Virginia on his way to the battle of Chattanooga, only to get there too late and not see him at all.

Some of the most impressive passages contained in the letters are those referring to Eli's religious faith. There were a few instances when this faith appeared to falter, particularly after some terrible battle in which he was involved, but he very quickly regained hope, renewing his affirmation of faith, with confidence that he was truly in God's hands.

This family has become very real to me, and as you read this account of Eli Landers' war experiences, with quotations from his letters, I hope it will become real for you as well. As I have done, I hope you will also develop respect for this young man who fought for the cause of freedom as he understood it.

From its inception, this book was meant to be Eli Landers' story and the part he played in the War for Southern Independence. Yet, his family played such a prominent part in his life that they cannot be ignored in the telling of Eli's story. Even though I am now publishing this book, my search will continue for other links in the family chain. I still have hopes of finding a picture of Susan, who Eli said was the "best mother in the world." I also hope to find relatives of his beloved sister, Caroline, whose life led her to Mississippi. Each week, it seems that another Landers relative makes themselves known to me and the ones I have already met have become very good friends. so, I, in turn, must thank Eli for sharing his family with me.

## ACKNOWLEDGMENTS

Now that this manuscript has been completed, there are some people I would like to thank for helping make it a reality.

I am indebted to Nellie and Ricky Mobley for sharing Eli's letters with me so that his story could be told.

For many kindnesses and help in researching Eli's roots, I owe a great deal to the Landers family members in Georgia and Alabama. I would particularly like to thank Evelyn Kent Mays of Lilburn, Georgia who was the first member of the family to respond to my request in the Gwinnett *Daily News* for information.

For fulfilling Eli's request for a special tombstone and for providing his memorial service, I would like to thank all the members of the 5th Mo/9th Ga regiment of re-enactors of Lilburn, Georgia. Particular thanks are extended to Jimmy and Theresa Dodd for their work in organizing the activities of the memorial weekend.

For the practical help in the early stages of production of this book, I am indebted to Joe Sherrill of Martin Community College for his patience and untiring efforts in assisting me meet my deadline.

Special thanks go to artist Stephen McCall for his impressive drawings. He alone could have transformed my inner vision of Eli's story into the wonderful renderings that you see in the pages of this book.

I also wish to express my gratitude to Don and Ann Torrence of Williamston, North Carolina for having faith in my dream and for making it possible for Eli's story to be published.

Lastly, I wish to thank my friend and editor, Thomas Williams of Washington, North Carolina for his faith in my manuscript and for his expertise in breathing life into it.

*My Respected Mother,*

*I went up in town today and got my ambertype taken which I will send to you and I want you to keep this one for me and believe it to be the same boy that left you. This one cost 3 dollars but you won't take $100 for it when you get it. Mamma I want you to keep my picture as long as you live and show it to all the girls. Tell them that it is a Virginia Ranger. It is just like me now so you can guess how I look. "It" tells the girls and you all howda for me. It can't talk with you but if I was there I could tell you a heap! Look on the cartridge box and you will find my name which was put there with a lead pencil. So keep this picture My Dear Mother for it is just like I am now. Remember that it is a son of yours who is in the noble cause of his country and who will willingly stay with it till death if needed!"*
                                                        —Eli Landers to Susan Landers

Gather around your country's flag,
Men of the South the hour has come—
None may falter, none may lag—
March to the sound of, the fife and drum.

**Confederate States of America.**

Dear Mother in complianc6 with your special request I am at a loss to no what to Tell you for I dont wish to deceive no Boddy as for Being regenerated By the holy sperit of god I cant say that I have ever Bin But for the past 2 months I have Bin in some degree pestered from what caus I cant Tell But my weak efforts seems like chaff Before the wind But I have resolved if I Die an go to Hell By the help of god to do Better in my future life than Iv don in the past I feel it a debt that I owe to lead a more quiet life But many Trials meet me on the way we have meeting hear ever night & sunday it seems to have a great tendancy ther way 11 Baltized last sunday without I could give more satisfaction to you a few words will Be Best But Remember me in your petitions let no one out of the family see this for I fear it is all stuff So farewell Dear Signed E, P, Landers

A letter of Eli Landers to his mother

# Chapter I
# Leaving Home

IN 1861, HOWELL COBB, who had served as governor of Georgia in 1851, was serving as president of the Provisional Congress of the Confederacy in Montgomery, Alabama. When the decision was made to move the capital to Richmond, he decided to organize a regiment of Georgians which he could take with him. In that way, he reasoned that he could serve not only the Confederate Congress as its president but could command a regiment as well.

He had joined the army because he thought it would have a positive effect on the people of North Georgia who had resisted secession for so long, and since he had largely talked them into seceding, Cobb felt obligated to take an active part in the fight. Cobb began recruiting in early June of 1861 and on July 15th had received a commission at the rank of colonel in the Confederate army. By the middle of August he had successfully raised a full ten companies of volunteers with orders to report for service in Richmond as soon as possible.

The companies organized in Gwinnett County were the Flint Hill Grays and the Hutchins Guards. Cobb's full unit became the 16th Georgia Regiment of Infantry, and he chose Lt. James Barrow to serve as his staff adjutant. Lt. Barrow's reputation as a good officer preceded him in the Georgia countryside and helped make the recruiting of men for the 16th Regiment much easier than it normally would have been.

Another factor contributing to the willingness of the men to enlist was their desire to get into the war before it was all over. The Union defeat at the First Battle of Manassas had led them to believe that it would be a very short war. One of the

recruits in The Flint Hill Grays, Co. H of the 16th Regiment of Georgia Volunteers was a young boy from Gwinnett County named Eli Pinson Landers. He lived on a farm with his widowed mother, Susan Landers, and his young sister Caroline. He had two married brothers, Humphrey and Napoleon, and three married sisters, Elizabeth, Harriet, and Rebecca Adaline.

Eli's father was one of four sons who migrated south from Virginia through North and South Carolina to Georgia in the early 19th century. Probably originating from Scotch-Irish stock, they had always been used to working hard for everything they had, asking nothing from any man. This was true, too, of Eli's immediate family, who in a time of slavery, had no slaves to help tend their North Georgia farm of wheat, cotton and corn.

Eli's devotion was always to the cause of Southern independence, however, and not for the forced servitude of slaves. "I would like to be at home but I can't for it is Dixie Land I am sustaining and I will live or die on the Frontiers of Dixie. Remember that I am a son of yours who is in the noble cause of his country who will willingly stay with it till death if needed." The Landers family was a close knit one. Eli's love for them is reflected in the note he hurriedly wrote to his brother before leaving on the morning of August 11th.

*This is the 11th day of the month and I must write some more to let you know that the time has come close to hand when I must close the old cottage door. They are now getting breakfast. When I eat I will start to the Stone Mountain to leave there at half past 9 o'clock tonight. If nothing happens I will eat my breakfast in Augusta in the morning and I will mail this letter today at the Mountain. But we have a fine set of boys. All of our Settlement boys but Bill Miner. Tell Barry Brasell that he has missed the best chance in the world. My hand and heart trembles so this morning that I can't write much as I would for the thoughts of leaving Gwinnett and my Mamma and friends in general. I have said nothing about domestic business in my letter nor don't expect to. My time is short here. Breakfast is nearly ready and then I must start. But if I never see you again take care of yourself and I will try*

*to do the same. So no more only truly remain your affectionate*
*brother until Death.*
*E.P. Landers to H.D. Landers*

On the day of his departure, Eli's brother Napoleon and
his brother-in-law, Moten accompanied him to Stone Mountain
where his journey north to Richmond began. This was probably
the first time he had ever been away from home, and Eli
described how he felt that day as he left his friends and family
who went to see him off:

*Dear Mother,*

*You spoke of something in your letter that has crossed my*
*mind many times since I left home. That was how I looked*
*though I never said a word that morning that I left. I tell you*
*I was past speaking. I never was so heart stricken before now*
*but only God himself knew my feelings when I left the gate and*
*they can never be expressed. It is anomating to think of the way*
*the people done at the mountain that night we started. It was*
*bad to part with friends but God bless them is my prayer if I*
*never see them again. Tell Moten and Pole I have not forgot*
*how they stood round the car by me but I rolled from them fast!*

The men traveled by train to Augusta, where they were
warmly welcomed by the local citizens. Eli described their
reception in his letter of August 15th:

*We ate breakfast in Augusta Monday morning. We got there*
*about sunrise. The citizens of Augusta give us our breakfast*
*and treated us well. There was a young lady give me a flag*
*made of silk ribbon and told me to take it to Virginia but some*
*grand raskal stold it. The people, both men and ladies, give us*
*the praise all the way. They hurahed for Georgia for she carrys*
*the day here at Conier's Station. The tracks was full of ladies*
*and fellas. I fell in love with one of them. She had on a dress like*
*Add's white one.*

From Augusta they crossed into South Carolina and

traveled to Charleston where he described crossing a bridge that was, he said, three miles long and twenty five to forty feet high. The troops then traveled on north to Wilmington, North Carolina where they had to get off the train and cross the Cape Fear River by steamboat.

Eli described the river as being about one and a half miles wide at their point of crossing. After the crossing, they boarded a train again and proceeded north on the Wilmington-Weldon Railroad line through Kinston to Petersburg, Virginia, where they spent the night in a house that had been appropriated for their use. It is interesting to note that at that date, Petersburg was a much larger city than Atlanta. Eli noted that "Atlanta is just a baby compared to this town." The train finally reached Richmond the next day, and the wide-eyed youngster from Georgia immediately wrote back home to share the marvelous sights he was seeing.

> *I can set here and look out yonder in the field and see 1000 men drilling one squad. There are about 13,000 men campt at this place. I walked out on the field yesterday evening and saw Colonel Sim's Regiment drill. It was the prettiest sight I ever saw. We put up our tents yesterday evening and it looks like a little town. I reckon there are a thousand tents here. I can't write much but I could tell you a heep if I could see you. There is one regiment now leaving here to go to Fare Creek. The artillery is now saluting them by firing cannons. They have fired five times. I saw the artillery yesterday evening with their wagons and cannons. You can't hear nothing but drums and fifes here hardly. They have got lots of prisoners in Richmond. I am going back into town today to see them. I could write more but everything is so confused. This old war is opened up at last and thank God for it. It will be Death or Victory but if to the latter, I want them to either fight it out or quit one. So help me pray for a fight or peace. I never expect to see you till I can land home in honor for that is the only way that I ever expect to see old Gwinnett. I expect to stand my hand in the Cause as long as I can for I am now sold to Jeff Davis and I expect to serve him till he discharges me in honor or till I die!*

Eli's break with home was now a complete reality although the pain of leaving for the first time was assuaged by the excitement of seeing new places and meeting new people. The air in Richmond was electric with talk of impending battles with the "hated enemy from the North." Eli's natural enthusiam, however, would soon wane as the tedium of daily living set in.

## *Chapter II*
## *The First Camp*

THE SIXTEENTH REGIMENT arrived in Richmond on the morning of August l4th, 1861 and set up Camp Cobb at the Old Fair Grounds, which was about a mile from downtown Richmond. In his first letter home from Richmond, Eli still spoke of the war as a"lark". "Tell Bill Miner," he wrote," that he will miss all the fun if he don't come, and tell So Turner that we have got away from our families at last." His next letter was full of excitement as he described the camp to his mother:

*Dear Mother,*

*This morning after coming back from drilling I am much wearied. I seat myself to tell you that I am in my tent by myself and to tell you that I am well this morning. I promised you that I would write you the truth if I could but it is impossible to do it although I am allowed to write what I please. When I wrote you the first letter I had just got here and had not seed much then but my eyes has been opened since then. We moved from that first campground to the Old Fair Ground. There is about 5 acres in it. They keep guard out all the time and we can't pass out nor in without taking a pass from the Captain. It is hard for a white man to tote a written pass like a Negro! The Gwinnett Negroes is free compared to us but don't tell Bill Miner that! Let him come on up here. There is two fellas just come out of the guardhouse. They was put in there night before last. I wrote to you that it was cold here and it was, but in the*

*morning it got as hot a day as I ever experienced. The sweat is running down my cheeks right now. We have had enough to eat till last night. We did not have a bit of bread for supper, only what we bought because the quartermaster drawed rations for five days and it give out. I got permission from my captain and went up in town. There I saw the greatest place I ever did see! Atlanta is nothing more than a kitchen to a Big House. I will tell you folks that there is no use in trying to compare nothing to what I have saw since I left home. I saw Washington's Monument. It was away up a stack of fine rock and he is on the largest horse that I ever saw. Washington is on the horse with his sword in his hand. The horse and man looks as natural as nature itself. Just get out of the way because it looks just like its coming right onto you! It is larger than any man or horse you ever saw I also shook hands with old Zachary Taylor yesterday evening. He looks just as natural as the man itself. It is about the size of a man and is made of tombstone. You can see the coat buttons and neck tie, even down to his shoe strings. Well, I really can't tell you as plain as it is. Here we are 750 miles apart and I am here trying to tell you the conditions! We expect to be called tomorrow as soon as we get drilled enough but we are ready to start anytime. They had a fight in Missouri on the 16th. We killed and wounded three or four thousand and was still in pursuit of them with a large body of cavalry and was likely to destroy all of them which I am in hopes they will. They had a fight in thirty two miles of us on Wednesday night. The Yankeys killed and wounded five hundred of our men but we whipt them in the fight. We don't know how many we killed of them but they drove fourteen hundred of the Yankeys up in Richmond "to take supper with us!"*

Before the young men enlisted, the Southern journalists of the day told the Confederates not to fear the Yankees because they were "a dimunitive race of feeble constitution, timid as hares, with no enthusiasm and would perish in short order under the glow of the Southern sun." Eli described them quite differently however, saying

*I met up with twenty two hundred of my enemies yesterday*

*evening but they was prisoners. They was stout looking fellers. Tell the People back home to quit talking about "Little Yankeys" for they are Big Devils and do look so mean that I could not help from cussing them. I just shook my fist at them and they did look at us so mean. I saw them come out to go to get water. Some was barefooted and some without a shirt. There was one man stood off and curst them of the meanest devils that he could think of.*

Southern soldiers thought of the Union soldiers as being inferior, coming from a low and vulgar background. They also thought of them as being deceitful and tricky. In an undated letter Eli cited an instance of Union trickery which destroyed a regiment of Floridians:

*A New York Regiment hoisted a Confederate flag and hollered for help. A Florida Regiment went to their assistence taking*

*Richmond Va*

*them to be their friends and when they went as close as the Yankees wanted them, they began to fire on them, the Floridians finding them to be their enemy. They let in on them and slain nearly everyone of them that was shot. If they get by with such undermining tricks I don't know what we will all do. It looks like they have sot into whip us but maybe it's all for the better. The hotter the war-the sooner the peace!*

A letter to Eli from his mother revealed the negative feelings that the average Southerner back home harbored concerning the Northerners:

*Eli, you needn't be uneasy about us for we are surrounded with Christian friends while you are there with Yankeys and if we never meet in this world I want us to try to meet in a better one.*

Eli's letter about his first impressions of Richmond continued:

*The drum has beat and I must get in line or else be imprisoned 24 hours in the guardhouse. Thom Sanders was absent the other night and he was kept in the guard house a night and a day. Write and tell me how the crops look and if it has rained any there or not. We have plenty rain here. It has been half shoe mouth deep round our tent but it is drying up, but there is a likely prospect for more rain. Mamma don't let none of this trouble you for I have just reconciled to my lot. I want you to write to me as often as you can. You know what I want to hear. Tell all the girls to write for I would like to hear from all my old friends. This letter closes with thoughts in Gwinnett. Truly remaining your affectionate son until death.*

In only a few days time he was saying how glad he was to get out of "Miss Cody's cotton patch", but the initial glow of freedom had already dimmed." We are in this place and can't get out," he wrote," We are like birds in a cage but I have given myself up to Providence and I hope I will be present both soul and body."

Susan Landers

*"Mamma, it made me feel awwful bad when I received your ambertype. It looked so natural and just to think who it was and where the original of it was. Money couldn't get it! W.T. smith put it in his trunk. Hed says he will take care of it 'till the Yankees take it from him."*

*Letter of October 9, 1861*

At this time, the men of the regiment were allowed to elect their own officers. The volunteers were very proud of having this privilege, and the election was a big event in their lives. In some units, the soldiers would elect the man who had raised their regiment, while in others there would be a highly competitive race with much ill feeling resulting. Sometimes the man who lost would ask for transfer to another company. Eli said that his regiment had nominated Ben Gober to be its Captain but he only received 18 votes while his opponent Ben Gholston received 54 votes. Even though his candidate was not elected, Eli seemed to be satisfied with the choice. This practice of electing officers was later abolished as officials began appointing the best qualified men for the job. In his letter of September 5th, Eli wrote:

> *Ben Gholston is our captain now. You can just all think what you please about Captain Richardson and his company that he has forsaken, well think the same. If we had followed our captain we woulda been in Gwinnett now but he was a solger for money.*

Records indicate that Richardson enlisted with the regiment on August 11th and resigned on September 3rd, serving only twenty three days. Since it was permissible to hire someone to fight in your place, it is possible that this is what he did. The soldiers' opinion of this practice is apparent however, from the tone of Eli's letter. Later in the war, Eli wrote about a member of his company, identified as "John A.", being disappointed since the authorities would not take a Mr. Walker as a substitute for him. He was according to Eli, "Much perplexed at the thought."

The men were separated into small groups, each of which was called a "mess." A mess was generally composed of from five to ten men who grouped themselves according to similar tastes and associations, long-time friendships, or by kinship. In Richmond, Eli's mess was composed of his cousins, Archibald and Elijah McDaniel, Bob and Thom Matthew, Jim and Ben Traynham, John Walas, Dave Cruse, and Dave McGinnis, his brother-in-law. They were responsible for cook-

*"Everything is silent at this time. No prospect for an immediate engagement here. We are enjoying a good long rest which we all very much needed."*
Spotsylvania Cty. Va.
August, 1863

32

ing their own food and brought their own cooking utensils,
camp kettles, frying pans, bread trays, water buckets, and
spoons. When they first got to Richmond, the food was plentiful with rations of meat, bread, rice, sugar, and coffee, but within
only about two weeks time the men had to buy their own bread.
On one occasion, twenty two of them pooled their money and
hired an old Negro man to cook for them for one week. He
cooked beef dumplings and bread among other things. They
divided the cost of the cook's services -seventeen and a half
cents for each man.

*"Today we had a good cake and coffee and molasses and fried taters, but didn't have a clean tablecloth to put on of a Sunday morning! It is every man gets his handful and stand round and eat it, for if a fellow stands back he gets none."*
October 6, 1861

Eli told of the crowded conditions in his tent which he
shared with five others. He said they were so badly crowded
that they had to get up and go out of doors to turn over, but they
did the best they could. Later they found some boards and built
a floor that was more comfortable than the cold ground. When
they were out in the field, Eli wrote, they did not always have
a tent but shared an oilcloth which they spread on the ground
and then covered up with two blankets and another oilcloth.
This arrangement was not the best, but it did keep them fairly
dry in snow or rain. Each man was issued twelve pounds of
straw a month for a bed on the ground when tents were not

*"The rain was half shoe-mouth deep around our tent."*
August 18, 1861

33

available. Eli made several requests for an oilcloth to be sent him from home. His mother answered his request in a letter of October,1861:

> *We could not send you anything with Wright but a half gallon of brandy. It was in the jug with Bob Miners in W.T Smith's box. I would a sent you an oilcloth but Jim and Uncle Ely went and got theirs before I knew it and they said when you stand guard Arch and Lige would lend you theirs and I was scarce of money and had to pay the cash for your shoes.*

The official Confederate uniform had a double breasted gray tunic with two rows of buttons. The collar and cuffs were trimmed in red, blue, or yellow to designate the branch of service (Blue,Infantry; red,artillery; yellow,cavalry). It had light blue pants and sometimes a gray flannel overcoat with cape. It was completed by a small cap, black necktie, and black boots.

This was the official uniform, but many different ones were seen on the battlefield. A large majority of the soldiers had to provide their own clothes since the Confederate government was unable to provide uniforms for them. They usually wore whatever they had and oftentimes they did not have nearly enough. Eli began writing home for additional clothes almost as soon as he reached Richmond. He mainly asked for flannel drawers and woolen caps. In September he asked for a long frock-tailed coat that would come to his knees to protect him when it was raining. Later in October he began asking for flannel shirts, buckskin gloves,shoes, and blankets. Shoes and blankets were very often in short supply since both wool and leather were difficult to obtain. The lack of shoes was the most serious problem for the infantryman, causing much straggling among the ranks, oftentimes making them late arriving at their duty stations.

Eli's mother answered his request for clothing with a letter in October:

> *We could not get your pants ready and as for flannel there aint none to be had about here. We will send your pants when we*

*"Eel, I want to know if you got them apples I sent you or not. I sent them in your coat pocket because there was eight of them."*
Caroline to Eli,
October, 1861.

34

This building housed the Yellow River Post Office, which was established in 1846. Families gathered here during the Civil War to get mail from their loved ones on the front. Many of Eli's letters were addressed to the Yellow River Post Office. Below, an envelope cover from Eli Landers.

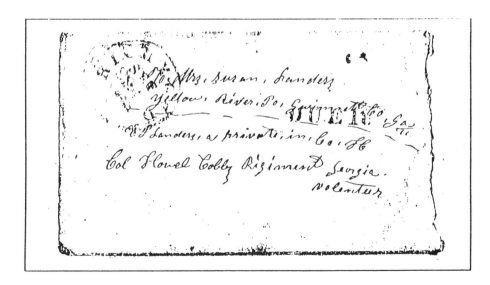

*A quire of paper
is 24 sheets*

*do your shoes or boots too and I want to know which you had ruther have, boots or shoes. Write which soon and I will get Tect to make you some. If times was not so hard you should have arry thing you wanted. Bacon is 30 cts a pound, molasses 60 cts, paper 50 cts. a quire and none hardly at that. Coffee is 2 pounds to the dollar but our country don't make much use of it. Calico is 20 and 25 cts a yrd but everybody is wearing cotton dresses.*

*"We expect to be at Manassas Junction in a few days. The Colonel has sent his horse off to get him shod this morning to be ready."*
September, 1861

*"There is no prospect for peace that I can see but we don't know no more about it than you do. You may think that because I am in Virginia I know all about the war but I tell you I con't for we don't get the chance to run about."*
September, 1861

After the boys got into the routine of long marches and a shortage of soap and water, the uniform underwent some modifications. The boots were found to be cumbersome and heavy so brogans became the preferred footwear. The long coat was too bulky and was replaced by a short jacket. The buckskin gloves, once in such demand, were found to be a nuisance since they hampered one's ability to shoot a gun. Eventually, it would come down to one man, one shirt, one pair of pants, and one pair of drawers. There was simply no place to store extra clothes and no soap with which to wash them. From the very beginning of the war, payment of wages to the soldiers was not made on a regular basis. Eli drew his first pay on the fifth of September. It amounted to a total of $7.70 and covered the time from August 11th, when he left home, to the first of September. The men were informed that there would be no more money until December at which time they would receive $33.00. Eli said that his brother-in-law was being paid $18.50 a month for driving a wagon. Half that amount, he said, was being paid to regular foot soldiers. He later wrote that he had been able to draw two months wages but that the government still owed him one hundred dollars in back pay, plus the fifty dollars "bounty money" that would soon be due. In June of 1862 he was so in need of money, he wrote, that he sold a pair of his pants for six dollars. He complained that "Money is as scarce as hen's teeth." It was so scarce in fact, that if a soldier's pay was due on the day of a battle, the quartermaster would not pay him until after the battle in case he were to get killed and the money "go to waste." By early fall of 1861, the Union blockade of the Southern coast was beginning to show its effectiveness in keeping out much needed supplies from England. The 16th

Regiment had received orders to move out on the Peninsula to Yorktown to assist in the recapture of Fortress Monroe from the Federals, but they had no guns with which to fight. In the first week of September, Colonel Cobb received news that the blockade runner *Bermuda* had slipped through the Union lines with Enfield rifles from England as well as some from Germany and he sent a requisition to Savannah for enough rifles to equip his regiment. His order was denied however, because Governor Brown of Georgia had impounded the rifles. Eli mentioned this lack of guns in his letter of September 15th:

> *Mother, I have not much to write only I will have to leave this place next week. We will go to Yorktown about 75 miles from this place. We expect to have to take Fortress Monroe. They say there are forty thousand Yankeys there. The companies that has got guns is ordered to march right away but our company has not drawed any guns yet We will draw them next week. They will be the old fashion musket.*

A week later he wrote that the guns still had not arrived:

> *We are still at Richmond but we are looking everyday when we will start to Yorktown. The Vice-President made us a speech the other evening. He said that he would insure us to be well armed in the course of the next week and then we will march immediately, but I am willing to go.*

On October 14th he wrote:

> *The report is that we will get our guns today and leave here Wednesday for Yorktown but I don't know whether it is so or not for there is so many reports in camp that I don't know when to believe anything.*

The reports were true. After Cobb registered an official complaint over the delay in arming his men, the guns were finally shipped by the middle of October. To his dismay however, the rifles were so rusty when they arrived that they could not be used and it took another week to replace them with

*"I was in hopes that this war would soon close but from the reading of the late papers I think we may lay down all hopes of peace and prepare for an Everlasting War. I am afraid that we are a ruined Nation, but let us not be disheartened for all things must work out to the Will of God."*
Undated

others that were in working condition. Colonel Cobb used this delay productively to learn what was expected of him as a field officer, since prior to this time he had been a mere politician without military training. The guns were good ones and apparently worth waiting for, and it was said that Cobb had the best armed regiment in the Confederate army

Mail delivery began to be a problem. Many times stamps were not available and letters had to be hand delivered by someone who was going back home. In some cases it seems that one or two people from each home community had the express job of serving as a delivery agent since the same name appears in several of Eli's letters as that of the person who was delivering the mail. "I will send this by a man going from here this evening to his Lawrenceville home. I must fix it up in such a hurry that I don't expect you can read it, and again I will send this letter by Mr. Hutchins to Yellow River."

This method of delivering mail was not a particularly efficient way, and Eli was already complaining about not hearing from home after having been in camp for only two weeks: "I have wrote three or four letters back home and have never received a line from none of you yet but I will write to you later if I never hear from you again. Out of so many of you it looks like I could get a letter! I want you to write soon as you get this for I want to hear from you all before I leave this place for I may not hear from you any more for the Yankeys is as thick as hops down about where we are going.".

Maintaining contact with home through letters was very important to the boys. "As long as I can get letters from you or any of my friends," Eli wrote," I can do very well but when I can't hear from you all I begin to feel a long ways from home and that you all have forgotten me." He asked for the most minute details about the family and farm operations so that in a sense he could be a part of it even though he was many miles away and in an alien land.

Much of Eli's correspondence to his mother and sister consists of instructions on tending the farm and how to do the chores once delegated to him. There was, too, a concern for his family's well-being in his absence:

*Mamma, I think perhaps you had better hire some person to work a while to fix the ground and plant the crop and get everything started and regulated for it is too rough for you and Caroline to undergo without you was well. I don't know how you will make out by yourself nor how you will save the wheat but if there is any chance I want you to save it all. Speak to Mr. Arnold and see if he won't cut it for the wheat or the money. Caroline I can hardly keep from crying of you and Add having to swing the plow but I can't help it. You must be careful with the horses and don't run too close nor too fur from the corn and write how your garden patch looks. I want you to write Mamma and write long letters like you was talking to me. Write how things stands about home and how my filly is getting on. Take good care of her for she is all I have got. Tell Moten to break the little steers for it may be that I will be with him and if I don't, tell him to not forget me nor to write. Mamma I want you to write and tell me how you saved the fodder and how much you saved. I want you to take care of yourself because I am out of reach. Write how all the girls look and if they have many beaus now. Tell them to wait for us solgers, for the Virginia girls don't suit us.*

*Mamma I want you to write if you got them two dollars that I sent or not and write everything that you know. Write a long satisfactory letter. If you can't send it in one letter, send it in two. Tell all to write. Caroline I want you to write to me and write about everybody and everything for I love to read your letters. I don't know whether you like to read my letters as good as I do yours or not. If I knew that you did I would write oftener than I do. Mamma write if you think you will make enough corn to do you or not and how big is the biggest potatoe that you have got. Mamma, take care of my mare.*

His mother answered this last letter with the following remarks:

*You wanted to know how large the largest potatoes we got. We have got some as large as your leg but all the rows next to the*

*"Tell Jane I said God Bless Her and may the Devil Miss Her."*
September, 1861

ditch soured. I do wish you had some. We are trying to sell the mule. Yancey Cruse says he thinks we can get fifty dollars for it. He is to speak to Cruse about it though money is very hard to come by. We will try to sell it at some price for our corn crop will come off short."

His sister wrote him saying: "Eel, if you knowed how bad I wanted to see you you would run away and come home. Let me tell you about your mule. It come in the house today. It is the tamest thing you ever saw."

One of the most difficult things the troops had to deal with in those first few months, and indeed throughout the war, was the prevalence of disease among them. In fact, during the entire war one out of three deaths was caused by disease, principally dysentery and diarrhea. In the fall of 1861, three hundred men of the 16th Regiment alone, had "chills and intermittent fevers" caused by epidemics of measles and mumps. In the years 1861 and 1862, malarial fever accounted for one seventh of all sickness. In August of 1861, typhoid fever broke out in the camp in Richmond. It subsided in December of that year but raged again in September of 1862. Smallpox broke out in October of 1862 with a very high mortality rate. Other diseases which appeared at this time were pneumonia, tuberculosis, rheumatism, scurvy, and venereal disease. In two months, from August to October, the 16th Regiment had lost 30 men to these illnesses. These epidemics were thought to have been caused by the rural boys' lack of immunity, since they had never been out of the South and had not been exposed to these diseases.

News of the crops back home: *"My present tax is 4 dollars besides the war tax. It will be 8 or 10 dollars....Your sow had 5 nice pigs. Our hogs all looks well. Your mare looks mighty well, too. She is so petted. Moten has not broke your steers yet but will shortly. Pole and Moten is gathering our corn on the piece next to the meeting house. It never made 4 loads but that is good to what a heap of people up land has."*
Susan Landers to Eli Lancers, October, 1861

Other contributing factors were the inadequate diet, impure water supplies, exposure to the rain and cold, and lack of sanitation. Sickness broke out in the ranks of the 16th regiment within two weeks of its arrival in Richmond. On August 29, 1861, Eli wrote that there were at least 100 men in his regiment that were sick, including all the commissioned officers except one. He also mentioned the beginning of the measles and mumps epidemics that would grow progressively worse during the next two months. By September 5, the deaths had already begun. The sick soldiers had very little faith in the camp

40

hospital. Whenever possible they would go into the city and look for a family to take them in their home while they convalesced. Cobb did not like for his men to do this since he felt it was an imposition on the citizens of Richmond. He would not issue passes to men who he thought were going into town for that reason. Eli wrote to his mother describing the situation:

*Times is bad here and getting worse. There is so much sickness here that there is about 250 sick in this regiment. They are dying dayly. There has been about 15 died since last Sunday morning Last Thursday there was six that died. Two died in about fifteen minutes between their deaths. Though I have not been sick but one day since I left home, the sick is just lying thick through the camps on a little straw with their knapsacks under their heads It's like Brutus to see a man die on such places but they can't help theirself for Colonel Cobb won't allow them to be moved out of camp if he can help it but the most of them gets their friends to go out and get a house for them and then we steal them off to the house. Five or six of our sick ones run off the other evening and went to private houses. We have about forty two sick in our company and we are badly wearied waiting on them. There has two of the Lawrenceville County died since we come here. Their names was Cadell and Underwood. Underwood died yesterday with the measels. I have not bin sick only with diarrhea but I am cooking every day when I'm able. Nicholas Shamblee is now in Richmond sick. He is at a hotel. I have not got the chance to go to see him yet but Asa Wright saw him and Bob is going to see him today. Lt. Gober is very bad off. W.T. Smith looks like a skeleton though he is getting better. We have had a very serious time since this time yesterday morning for we have witnessed the death of one of our fellow solgers to wit Thomas Sanders. He died with a relapse of the measels. He got most well of them and exposed hisself in the rain. His relapse was very hasty to death. He only lasted 5 days this last time. He died last night about 1 o'clock. It was a very solemn occasion. He was out of his senses all the time. I was detailed to wait on him 24 hours. It almost wearied me down for he was trying to skip off all the time. He said he was going home but the poor fellow will*

41

*return home with his eyes closed. Asa Wright will come home with him. The company all throwed in their little mite to send him home with all pleasure and I for one did. It was heart rending to hear the bitter cries of him. The poor fellow called his Mother often. He died very hard indeed. John Sanders is down with the measels now and it is doubted wheather he ever will get well or not. The sick sees hard times for they are lying in the hospital tents on some straw. God forbid that I shall ever spend my last days in such a place for it is awful to see the sick groaning on any such place. I was just thinking the other day about Sweetwater graveyards. I know it would make me feel bad to go over it and see the silent tombs of so many of my friends whom I have been with so often. How thankful I ought to be that I have not been numbered with them yet.*

His sister, Caroline, wrote to him later to tell him about his friend's funeral service "We was sorry to hear of you losing one of your fellow soldiers. We all went to his burying. I tell you it was solemn times with us all. There was a large congregation there but they did not open the coffin to let us see him. He was buried at Sweetwater. I intend to keep his grave nice. I want to know if you want to be brought home if you die. I want you to. I don't care what it costs."

His mother also mentioned the funeral in her letter of October 5th: "Eli,I do want to see you so bad. I wish my son well. It was heart rendering to hear the bitter crying of Mr. Sanders' people at the burying. It made me feel awful. I just thought if it was you!"

There was not much smallpox in the camp that first year of the war but it broke out soon after the Antietam Campaign, in September, 1862. It is thought that the smallpox germs were brought in from the northern territory on the clothing of the captured Yankees. The epidemic reached its peak in early 1863, and left many hundreds dead in the Southern army. It was difficult to get vaccine for the smallpox and many times the men would resort to removing a scab from an infected person and putting it on a cut place on their own arm. Eli speaks of his vaccination in a letter of February 1863 when he says that smallpox has broken out again and that he had been vaccinated the second time. In March he wrote to his mother about the discomfort he was suffering from the vaccinations:

*Dear Mother,*

> *I once more seat myself to write you a few lines which will inform you that I am in good health all except the effects of vaccination. I have almost the afflictions of Job from it. I had some kind of braking out and the vaccination has caused inflammation wherever I am broke out. I can hardly get about without difficulty.*

Eli's sickness actually began a few weeks after he arrived in Richmond, when he complained of having an upset stomach. By October 9th he was much worse:

*My Dear old Mother,*

> *This day I take great pleasure in answering your letter that I received this morning and also your affectionate features [Photograph]. I received them with the greatest of pleasure though it did not come to hand as you desired it to for I was not well though not very bad off. I reckon it is the cold. I can't hardly write for my hand is so numb though I think in a few days I will be ready for service but if I don't I intend to go out to a private house for I don't think that the hospital tent is fit for me to stay in as long as I can do better. I hant got much to write and feeling so bad you need not to expect much of a letter but I will do the best I can Mamma it made me feel awful bad when I received your Ambertype. It looked so natural and just to think who it was and where the original of it was, money couldnt get it. W.T Smith put it in his trunk. He says that he will take care of it till the Yankees takes it from him. I reckon you have all heard of Thom Sanders being dead. Now his Brother John Sanders is dead. He died yesterday morning. He is up town in a vault. They have sent his Father word to come after him if he wants to. Both of them went just alike. They was out of their head all the time. John only lasted two days after his relapse. He was getting well and he went out and got drunk*

*and then drank as much cold water as he wanted and the next morning he couldn't walk nor never did. He died in the same tent that Thom did. We are very doubtful of Alpherd Jim a living for he is very low. Mamma I would like to see you but I don't know how long it will be till I do for the infurnal Yankeys intends to try to wipe us out as they first said but I don't think that they never will do it for I think the Lord is with us and if He be for us then who needs to be agin us. The Bible says the Wicked fleeth when no man pursueth. It proved so in the cowardly rout at Manassas. You wanted to know if I needed any shoes. I don't need them now but I soon will and they will cost 6 or 7 dollars here. If you can I want you to send me a good pair of homemade ones. I feel so bad I will quit till morning. Eli is not able to finish this letter but wants it sent and I will close it by signing his name.*

E .P. Landers Signed by E.M. McDaniel

Shortly after this letter was written, Eli entered the home of the Pemberton family there in Richmond who had extended their hospitality to him during his illness. He wrote to his mother to tell her about his condition:

*My Dear Mother*

*I take this opportunity to write you a few lines to let you know that I am not well at this time but hope this may find you in better health than it leaves me in. I am sick at this time. I am out in a private house. I don't know what my spell will terminate into but I hope nothing very serious. I am treated as well here as if I was at home and had my mother to wait on me but its much better than being in them old tents on the ground like many of my fellow soldiers is. I have a good feather bed to lie on and much better attention than if I had of stayed in camps. My captain is very kind to me. He lets Arch or Lige or Pink come and stay with me every night and as often in the day as he can he comes to see me himself. I just stayed in camp till I found out I was a going to be sick and I got Lige and Sam Dyer to get me a place and I got a pass to go out and return in two hours and I pitched my place and aint gone back yet but I hope it wont be long till I can be with the rest of the boys. My captain knowed I was not acoming back but he was darent to give me permission to go out to stay. The colonel wont let his men out when they are sick. He says the hospital tents is good enough but I didn't think so. We have lost three men out of our company and I don't believe they would of died if they had of had a feather bed and a good house to lay in and good attention. I am staying at Mr. Pemberton's. They are very kind to me. The reason I didn't stay at Mr. Hix is that one of his daughters is sick with the fever and I didn't think I could get very good care there so I must close. Write soon.*

*E. M. McDaniel writing for E. P. Landers*
*Aunt Susan, you needent to be uneasy about Eli for I think he gets good attention where he is. E.M. McDaniel*

Eli entered the Pemberton home on October 13th and wrote many times of their kindness to him. After being in their home for only one week, he had begun to recuperate.

*My Dear Mother,*

*Today I am going to try to write you a letter to let you know how I am. I am getting better. I can walk about in the house. I have been sick nearly three weeks. I was taken with the measles but they did not hurt me much. My regiment has left me and gone to Yorktown. They left last Saturday morning about day. The doctors would not let nobody stay with me but I have done very well without them. I don't reckon that I will go to camp in three or four weeks if I don't get no backset for I want to be sound when I try it again for I will tell you that the camp is a rough place. The Pembertons treat me as well as they can and they tend to me like I was a child though I have to pay my way and I have not got the money to pay them now but they say to not mind that for if I didn't have a cent they would treat me as well as if I had one thousand dollars! They have took in about seventy soldiers since the war began. Write just as soon as you get this for I want to hear from you. I have thought of you often since I have been sick. Goodby for this time.*

*E.P. Landers to Susan Landers*

Eli's mother wrote to him soon after she received his letter expressing her appreciation for the care given him by the Pembertons:

*Dear Son,*

*With much pleasure I seat myself to write you a few lines to inform you that we are all well. I do hope this may find you in better health than you was when you sent that letter by Bill Cothren. I was so sorry to hear of you being sick. It almost broke my heart. Ely I feel so bad about you being sick that I can't hardly write. My best love and thanks to the people that you stay with. I do crave to be there to put my hand on your aching head and to wait on you but I hope that good woman will be a Mother to you. Give her my love and thanks. I hope the Lord will be your physician. Look unto Him. I hope He will raise you and let you return home and see us all again. Give Mr. and Mrs. Pemberton my humble thanks. I hope the Lord will reward them for it.*

Eli continued to write about the good care he was receiving at the Pembertons:

*Dear Mother,*

*This morning I take pleasure in writing to you to let you know how I am today. I am improving though I have had a bad time of it. The doctor did not think that I would get over it but I am getting along finely. John Peden stayed with me last night. Mamma don't be uneasy about me for I am at a good place. I have a good old motherly woman to look after me, plenty to eat and what is good I can walk about up and down the street. Yesterday I walked right smartly about 200 yards. Mamma I have to pay my board here and hain't got but about three dollars in my pocket. Though if I was at the regiment today I could draw two months wages. Miss Pemberton says they don't need a cent and that she would do all she could for me.*

*Don't trouble yourself about me for there is as strong a God here as there is in Georgia. I hope I will see you all again.*

Just as Eli began to improve, he had a relapse and the month of November was a difficult one for him. In his letters of November, he tells of his condition:

*My Dear Mother,*

*This morning I will drop you a few lines to let you know how I am. I am not as well as I was when I wrote my last letter. Since that time I have had a disease nearly like the mumps. It got in my secrets and I thought that I would be ruined. I suffered tremendously though I am now getting over that. I have had a hard time of it. I don't know now when I will go to camp. The Captain sent me word by old man Franklin to stay in Richmond till I get perfetly well for he says where they are now is no place for a sick man. They say it is a very cold wet part of the world. I don't believe that I will be able to stand the camp this winter for they are exposed and sent out on picket two or three miles from the camp on the bank of the waters where the wind can come from a long ways. I have been here five weeks today and I'm not near as well as I was two weeks ago. I don't know what I will do for I don't want to go to the hospital and even though I owe Mr. Pemberton money for staying here I don't think he will be particular about the money for he is a mighty fine old man. I think that they ought to give me a discharge but they say that a man must have some settled disease but I am not able for service like I am. Till I hear from you again.*

*E.P. Landers to Susan Landers*

*My Dear Mother,*

*I will write you a few lines to let you know that I am doing, tolerable well though I have had a hard time of it. I hope this will find you all well for health is a great blessing. I will go to camp next week I reckon if nothing happens, though I don't know whether I can stand the camp when I go or not. But I can try it. I am sorry to hear of you being so uneasy about me for it is no use. I will write you again when I go to camp, so I have nothing more to let you try to reconcile yourself to our lot in this world. Your picture is a great consolation to me. Don't be uneasy about me. If I can't stand camp and don't die, I will come home. So goodby for this time.*

*E.P. Landers to Susan Landers*

Eli's service record shows that he was sent home on sick leave the end of November, and he did not return to his unit until January of 1862. His constant worry was not being able to repay the Pembertons for their kindness, but in a letter to Susan, written before Eli's furlough, Mr.Pemberton had assured her that he wanted nothing in return for the care given to Eli:

*Richmond, Va  Nov 19, 1861*
*To Mrs. Susan Landers*
*Dear Madam,*

*Your son E.P. Landers has been at our home sick for some 5 or 6 weeks and from a remark I heard him make this morning I fear he has written to you for money to pay for his care and that you may sacrifice some property to send him money. I write to assure you that we do not wish you to do any such thing and that we are willing to share the last cent with him rather than he should suffer for anything or put you to any uneasiness or trouble on his account. Don't sell anything on his account but rest assured that he will not suffer for anything that can be had in this city for money so long as he will stay at our house. He has been very low and though he recovers slowly I think him out of danger and hope in a few days that you may hear of his entire recovery. I was not aware until this morning of his wanting an account of his board or I would have satisfied him that it's of no importance. Please to think of him just as you would if the case were different and I was sick at your house. I know he would have attended me. We have had no little pleasure in his company for we find him as much of a gentleman as any person we ever saw. He is no trouble and while I am away he is great company for my wife who really seems to feel like a mother to him.  I hope you will not feel uneasy about him nor sell anything to send money, as I know very well it would be a sacrifice without half its value. Please write him of our assurance that all is right. Yours with respect, William D. Pemberton, No. 15 Pearl Street,  Richmond, Virginia, In Care of Weston Williams.*

In his own correspondence, Colonel Cobb spoke of some friction between his men and the people of Richmond. The Georgians, he said, disliked the Virginians. However, Eli's letters to his mother about the Pembertons and the Hix family that he had met seemed to reflect an entirely different attitude: "That lady that I was telling you about still says she will attend to me if I get sick. Their name is Hix. They grumble at me if I don't go out to see them everyday. They say that I am just like their brother. She says she is coming to Georgia with me when I come home but if they don't come till I do, it will be a good while for there is no prospect that I can see if times don't get better. In another letter he tells about the ladies of Richmond bringing in nourishments for the sick. He wrote:

> *The people of Richmond is very kind to us. There is some ladies now in our camps with some nourishment for the sick. They depend on the Georgia boys. Them ladies that you inquired about are named Sarah and Katy Hix. They send their respects to you all. I make out like I think there is nobody like them and they think a heap of me."*

Eli's sister Caroline expressed her regard for the people of Virginia who had befriended him in her letter:

> *Extend our respects to Mr. Hix's family. Also tell the girls I will look for a letter from them. Tell them I want to know how they like the Georgia boys. I never can forget them. Tell them I would like to see them. Their names is highly esteemed in this settlement."*

To add to the misery of sickness, the men were plagued with the infestation of a parasitic mite that burrowed under their skin, causing them to itch violently. Its spread was difficult to control and Cobb had the infected men confined and their tents burned. Eli confirmed this in his letter of November 15, 1861:

> *Mr Mose Herrington and Bob Miner and the two Odom boys*

*has got the 7 year itch. They are put off from the camp a little piece in a tent to themselves and ain't allowed to stay about the other tents. Bob and Mose caught it from the Odoms. They say they brought it from home. The doctors is at work on them now.*

If the men had a minor injury or cold, they would usually doctor themselves instead of going to the hospital. They used cures they had known back home and would gather herbs from nearby woods. Eli tells of putting a "blister" on his cousin E.M.'s chest and giving him some powder which made him feel better. The "blister" was a remedy often used at this time for chest congestion. A glass cup was heated until it was extremely hot and was then applied to the chest area so that the heat could "draw" the congestion away from the lungs. Most of the time it only resulted in a large blister appearing on the skin with no change in the original condition. Eli's cousin Arch tells of treating his brother E.M.'s burned hand by wrapping it in dry flour for two days and nights and then applying a dogwood poultice.

One of the most common complaints among the men was diarrhea. The Philadelphia *Enquirer* printed a recipe for a home remedy which many of the soldiers used: 2 oz. Laudanum, 2 oz. Spirits of Camphor, 2 oz. Essence of Peppermint, 2 oz. Hoffman's Anodyne, 2 drachs. Cayenne Pepper, 1 oz. Tincture of Ginger. Mix together. Put 1 teaspoon in a little water or a half teaspoon repeated in an hour afterwards in a tablespoon of brandy.

The ingredients for this potion were sometimes difficult to obtain, and when one of the men went home on leave, he would usually bring back the necessary herbs with which to make the medicine. While Eli was home on sick leave, his cousin E.M. asked him to bring back some red pepper "to put in Buck", which was obviously the cayenne pepper called for.

Another problem that surfaced during the first few months in Richmond was the presence of a large number of prostitutes. Since Richmond was the center of government as well as the site of large-scale military activity it became a center for prostitution. This must have been a new experience for these boys from rural Georgia, who had probably never seen such women before. Though their religious training told them otherwise, many of them fell prey to these women of the street.

According to the historian Merton Coulter, Camp Cobb was purposely located about a mile from the center of the city so that the men could be close enough to enjoy the hospitality it offered, yet far enough away to prevent too much "enjoyment" of its pleasures. Coulter did not spell out the precise meaning of those words. However, one might surmise that he was alluding to the problem of prostitution. One wonders if Eli was among the "fallen" because of some comments he made to his mother in several letters:

> *I have not forgot your advice Mamma but there is heeps of temptations here.*

> *There is so many temptations to lead me away. Richmond is a place of wickedness. There is so many temptations and aggravations here that a person is often led astray. It looks like the solgers get worst. It's almost a Band of Wickedness.*

> *Mamma I have become oppressed in mind somehow here of late but I fear it is through no good somehow. I can't reflect seriously and candid enough upon the great important matter upon which my eternal welfare is based. Oh that I could feel more dependent than I do. I know that self righteousness can never be eternally accepted. We are commanded to become entirely self denial and I have found it impossible without the help of God to do so. I know that life is uncertain and death is sure a penalty of life or death to follow and shall I be numbered with the Cursed, God forbid. I feel that I have strayed far enough if I only knew how to return. Dear Mother, if my heart is too hard to yield pray that I may boldly and successfully lay hold of the Tree of Life and live and that I may spend the remainder of my life different from days past and gone.*

One of the worst effects of prostitution was the spread of venereal disease, which greatly increased whenever the troops were stationed near cities. Statistics show the greatest number of cases reported from July 1861 until the spring of the following year. This was due to the large concentration of troops in the Richmond area at this time and also because the discipline was not as rigid as it would be later on. The freedom to explore this new, exciting life led many of the young farm boys into these houses of ill repute.

As it became more difficult to get men to volunteer for service, it became necessary by April of 1862 to resort to the conscription of soldiers. Many of these men resented being forced to enlist and the volunteers who were already in service looked down on the conscripts. The historian Carlton McCarthy said that they were the most despised class in the army. Most of the volunteers, he said, could not bear the thought of having them for comrades and felt they were an insult to the flag. In the early days of war fever, many of the young men joined up quite willingly. However, not all the young men were so anxious to go, and must have been embarrassed as news came in from the front about the activities of the ones who had enlisted. In one of her letters, Caroline relates an incident at Sweetwater Church when she was showing off Eli's picture in his uniform. "Eel," she wrote," I showed all the girls at meeting your picture. They all thought it was so pretty. There was a good many at Meeting, but the young men was so guilty they stayed outdoors!"

Word reached the men in Richmond that the draft law would be in effect in Georgia by March 4th, 1862. However, the first act of conscription was not passed until the 16th of April, 1862. Eli stated that he was sorry it had to be, because most of the men would have already joined up if they hadn't been needed at home, and now they would have to leave for the army. On the other hand, he said that he wanted the ablebodied men who had no ties at home to come and do their part because they were no better than those who answered the first call to arms. He said he was proud that he and his friends had volunteered at the beginning of the war and did not have to be forced to defend their country. He expressed the hope that the draftees would come in with the resolution in their hearts to aim for victory or death. Eli refers to the conscripts in a derisive manner in several of his letters, reflecting the general feeling about them:"There is conscripts here now that can't double quick 50 yards!" Most of the volunteers thought that conscripts were second-rate soldiers and made life miserable for them when they first arrived in camp. The majority of them proved to be good soldiers however, and they eventually won the respect of the other men.

After that thrill of getting away from home for the first time and the excitement of seeing new and different places had worn off, the men began to reflect more often on what they had left at home as well as what unknown dangers lay ahead of them. The early letters showed this probably even more than those of the latter years of the war, because at the time they were written the men had not become hardened to the life they were having to live. Eli expressed these feelings in several of his letters:

> *I stood duty the other night when it was raining hard and I thought of my old feather bed at home.*

> *There is many trials and tribulations to undergo here but I prefer it before subjugation.*

> *Mamma I never shall forget the last time I saw you and all the rest of my people. I would sure like to see some of the old Gwinnett peach pealings and water millions (watermelons) rinds. We hardly ever get anything of that kind but we must make out without them. This letter closes with thoughts in Gwinnett. Mamma I dream about you all nearly every night. I drempt that you had come to see me and I was going about Richmond with you but I hope that the day will come when it will not be in dreams that I will be with you when we will set down round your table to eat in independent peace for that is the only way that I ever expect to eat with you again. My dear Mother this is a dreadful life but I feel reconciled to it for I believe that we are on the right side of the question. Mamma I think about you every hour in the day. I just think about you working so hard without me till I hardly can stand it. It was hard enough when I was there to help you but you must do the best you can. It is hard for you to do without me and for me to lie on my blanket but I freely do it for my freedom for I have no*

*freedom here. I must close. So farewell my dearest friend.*

To Caroline he wrote:

> *Caroline I was with you this morning about daylight but the Legion drum beat waked me up. I just had got home when the sound of the drum brought me back to camp again but I hope the day will soon come when I will be at home so the drums can't bring me back!*

Without encouraging words from home, the boys would have had a difficult time coping with the life they had to endure in the crowded camps. In an undated letter that was obviously written early in the war, Eli begins to show some despair:

> *To all my Brothers and Sisters in Gwinnett, one and all. I will write a few lines in great haste. I feel this morining like one alone. This morning I had to cook my breakfast and set down and eat it all by myself for all my mess was sick. I have been in fine spirits all the time till this morning but the gloomy prospect that hangs over our heads has rather trimmed my feathers. But not withstanding all those gloomy clouds arise I can't help but believe that there is a day ahead that some of us will send the echo of our voice in the valleys of old Georgia in triumphs of the Liberty and independence and that we may live in peace once more. But there is no telling when that day will come for no one knows how long this war will last. But it is as I said, just so long as the Enemy follows us and persecutes us. My Friends, let me only ask one kind thing of you Let it be an easy task sometimes to think of me. E.P.L. to you all*

Susan Landers provided great support for her son, even though it was painful having to see him suffer in the cause for freedom. Her strong faith in her God however, sustained them all during those trying days, and she tried so hard to share this faith with Eli:

*Weep Not for Me Dear Mother*

*I want you to call on the Lord and if you feel any evidence let me know it. I do wish I was there to do something for you but as it is I can only pray for you. Don't go back to camp too soon. I hope the Lord will be your friend for He is all our dependance. Look to Him for help.*


Before his ordeal would be over, Eli would need many such words of encouragement. As it was, he spent part of November and all of December at home on sick leave. It is well that he didn't know what the future held for him or he might not have returned to the camp.

## *Chapter III*
## *The Peninsula Campaign*

ANTICIPATING INVASION by way of the Peninsula, the Confederate officials gave orders to the 16th regiment to leave Richmond and head toward Yorktown so they could protect Confederate interests at Fortress Monroe. Since Eli was too ill to go with his unit, he was left behind. He would join them later when he had regained his strength.

The regiment left Richmond on October 19th, 1861, on a train which took them to West Point. There they boarded the ship CSS Logan, which transported them to Yorktown. The men had been confined so long in Richmond that they enjoyed the boat ride, taking pot shots at sea gulls flying overhead.

They were now part of General John Magruder's Army of the Peninsula. Their job here was to observe the Federal forces at Fortress Monroe. Rumor had it that the 16th would be used as a "flying regiment" which would find the enemy, hit them, and run.

The new camp was named Camp Bryan in honor of their commander, Goode Bryan, who had been put in charge of the regiment while Howell Cobb was home on leave. Building living quarters proved to be a difficult job. The weather was bitterly cold and there were constant snow flurries. As Colonel Bryan reportedly said, the wind was "strong enough to blow the horns off the head of a Billy goat." There were not enough wagons to use for hauling the logs so the men had to haul them from the woods by hand. Then they cut them as best they could since the sawmill was inopperative.

When Colonel Cobb returned from his trip to Georgia, he moved his regiment again to a place on the Williamsburg

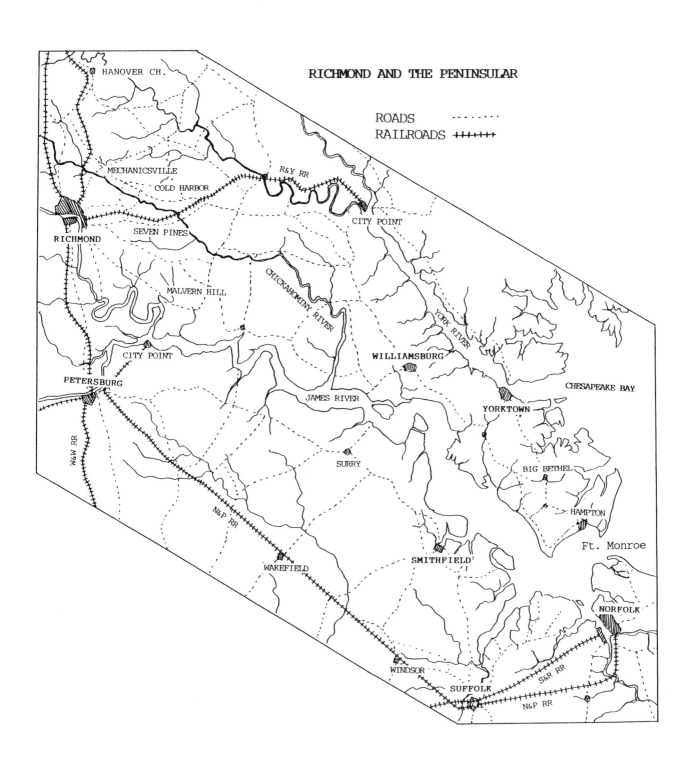

RICHMOND AND THE PENINSULAR

ROADS ·········
RAILROADS ┼┼┼┼┼┼

HANOVER CH.

MECHANICSVILLE
COLD HARBOR
R&Y RR
CITY POINT

RICHMOND
SEVEN PINES

MALVERN HILL
CHICKAHOMINY RIVER

YORK RIVER
WILLIAMSBURG

CITY POINT

PETERSBURG
JAMES RIVER
YORKTOWN
CHESAPEAKE BAY

W&W RR
SURRY
BIG BETHEL

HAMPTON

N&P RR
Ft. Monroe

SMITHFIELD
WAKEFIELD

NORFOLK

WINDSOR
S&R RR
SUFFOLK
N&P RR

Road about two miles from Yorktown. Since it was the custom to name the camps after family members, they named this one Camp Lamar in honor of Mrs. Cobb's brother. It was built on the ground where George Washington's men had camped before the surrender of Cornwallis. The men of the Sixteenth were comfortably housed in log cabins that were furnished with rough homemade furniture and shelves. Colonel Cobb described his cabin as a double one with each unit measuring 16 by 18 feet with a 10 foot connecting passage.

Eli's cousin Arch McDaniel wrote to him at home to tell him about the new living quarters that he would have when he joined them in Yorktown:

> *Eli you said that you wanted to know if we had divided our mess or not and wanted to know who was in it and wanted me to save you a place vacant in our tent which we have. We have built two houses for our mess. The Matthews Boys, Bob Miner and Wallis lives in one and us in the other. In our mess is me and Lige, Dave Mayfield and Nute Franklin. That's five and you will make six in one house. Ours is 10 1/2 X 12 1/2 feet and we have got shelves all round. Trup Liddleton said that we was very well fixed and that it looks very nice. Eli we will see a heap of fun here. I wish that you was with us but I don't want to hurry you back for you had better make good use of your time while you are there for if you ever get back you will know it.*

Even though the boys had little chance for courtship, they generally dreamed about the "girl back home." Oftentimes when someone went home for a visit he would be asked to deliver a kiss to the girl for the comrade left behind in Virginia. Arch requested this of Eli when he was home on leave:

> *I hope you saw a heap of fun with the girls and I hope that you did not forget that my mind was among you all. I hope that you kissed Paulina for me and told her what it was for and if you did not you do it before you leave. Tell her that I have not forgot her loving smiles and purty face. Eli, now don't take the start of me because I am not there to take my own part which I don't think you will but don't forget to kiss her and tell her that it*

*"Poor dependent people are deprived of the enjoyment of the pleasures at home that belongs to an independent people and the cussed invaders still trampling our homes and destroying our friends, seeking every way to bring us to entire subjugation. It is enough to raise the passion of all persons that claims the title of independent."*
E.P. Landers,
Undated.

*was for me. Then you may repeat it again if it suits her but I would rather that I was there to do it myself. I bet you and Bill Smith took the leeway with girls at old Sweetwater. You seemed to talk like that Cobb's Boys was the boys for the girls and I don't doubt it. If they had of had you as a sample of them they only had the dribble end of them. If they took on so about you, dropshot, I don't know what they would do if they could get a fare sample. I guess that they would hop round like a cat shot with hot fat! Enough of that!*

Eli returned to the camp at Yorktown around the middle of January, 1862. He had difficulty getting to the camp. They traveled by boat, and the water was so rough they couldn't land and had to wade ashore in the cold water. He wrote of his ordeal in a letter to his mother when he got back to the camp:

*Dear Mother,*
*All this evening I take pleasure in letting you know that I am at home and feel well as common. This is Monday and I got to camp last Saturday. I had good luck all the way till I got to Yorktown. But I come out safe. The boat could not land on the York side and we had to land at Gloucester Point. We could not get no place to stay that night and it was very cold and raining and there was no other chance to cross only in a small schooner. We went about 2 miles in a boat about 3 feet across the top. They could not get it to land for the tide was so high. We had to waid about knee deep. I got wet nearly all over and my slip of clothes and letters got wet but nun of them was ruined. We went out to the 6th Ga. Regiment and stayed all night. Luit Liddle stayed with Luit Culweel and I stayed with Bill Huff. The waves would raise the schooner high as my head and all appearance of danger showed itself. Luit Liddell was the worst scared man you ever saw. But it did not frighten me much for I just thought if we ever got to land we would be on the other side and if the waves wrapped us up I would not be by myself. I was afraid that it would make me sick but I feel no symptoms of it yet. Me and Liddell marched out next morning to camps about three miles through mud shoe mouth deep. We got to camp about 9:00. The boys was the gladest set of boys*

*you ever saw. I have not got through talking yet nor won't in two weeks. The boys is now drawing lasses [molasses] and they keep such a fuss about it till I can't write.*

Eli found that the food supply was much better than it had been when he left in November. He said:

*All the boys is well and hearty and are as fat as pigs. They have eat so much beef 'till they favor a cow. They throwed away enough beef the other day to make a good milk cow! Today we drawed flour and pork and molasses. We will live well 'till it is gone. I tell you the truth, we are well fixed.*

He also found much better living quarters than he had had in Richmond. As he explained:

*Mamma don't be uneasy about me for we are well fixed for living with a good log cabin dobbed as tight as a tater house. We are fixed just as comfortable when we ain't on duty as if we was at home. We have got a straw bed and plenty of blankets. I lay as comfortable as I ought to. I have been cutting wood today and that is all the duty I have done.*

Eli had stopped by Richmond before going to Yorktown to visit with the Pembertons who had taken such good care of him, and he told about them in his first letter home:

*I left the mountains at 9:00 on Monday night and rolled up to Richmond Wednesday evening at 6:00. I felt like I had gotten home and my folks were all very glad to see me. They was greatly surprised when I stepped in and applauded as glad to see me as if I had been their son. Next day I went down to see Cate. I was met at the door with a kiss. Tell W.T.Smith that Cate looks as well as ever. She read his letter with pleasure. There was two neighbor girls in that evening, Miss Liza Bie and her sister. I went home with Miss Liza and another fellow went with the other. Tell Liz that I got the Richmond girls' hearts! They all have great sympathy for the 16th Georgia Rgt. and especially for the Flint Hill Grays. They say we are the best soldiers in service. Mr. Pemberton said that he would answer your letter soon. Samp Garner stayed with me in Richmond and said they are the best people he ever saw. Before I left, I left ten dollars with Mr. Pemberton.*

Even though the Pembertons assured Eli and his mother that they did not expect payment for taking care of Eli, he felt honor bound to pay this debt that he felt was due his benefactor. He mentions his obligation to Pemberton in several more letters:

*The boys has all just drawed their money, two months wages but I will not draw any this time. I have not heard from Mr. Pemberton yet. I don't know what to think of the old fellow. I reckon that I can get enough money to make out on but I haint got but one dollar in the world but that don't make much difference for we don't need much only to get paper and stamps.*

In April he mentioned his debt to Pemberton again:

*Mamma, I just write this to let you know about that money. I hain't took the notion to send it when I wrote Ads letter and I haint paid Pemberton yet and if you get in a place that you need my money you may have it for he is able to do well without it.*

Those first few weeks in the new camp were pleasant ones for the 16th. Eli wrote home in high spirits telling about the comfortable cabins with the good fire that they were enjoying while it was snowing outside. He also reassured his family that he was feeling fine even though there was still sickness around him in the camp. This comfort would soon be broken, since already there had been reports coming into camp about enemy ships landing at Old Point, not far from their camp. They also had had orders to hold themselves in readiness for a march and to have their weapons in good working condition so that they could be ready to move at any moment. He described his situation in a letter to Caroline:

*Well H.C. as I have the chance of sending a letter by Luit Cain I will write you a few lines in a great hurry. This leaves me well and I hope that this may find you all well. I wrote you all a letter the other day sent by Capt.Hutchins. It is now a snowing as purty as you ever saw. We have a prospect for a heavy snow but we are comfortable in our cabins with a good fire. Tomorrow is my day to stand guard. I have stood guard once since I got back but it never hurt me. I have enjoyed very good health since I left home though A.W. is not well. He has got the yellow jaundice. Well H.C., I've no reliable news about the war. It is reported that there were several vessels of war landed at Old Point not far from here. This is sport, but orders came in the other evening to hold ourselves in readiness for a march and we fixed up our guns in order and are now ready at any minute to take the trip. Well all I have to say is just let them come along and then they will know how they get along. Well Car, you and all the rest of our folks must not think hard of me for not writing to you all individually for I don't have the time for this work to do another thing. Paper is very scarce. If I fail writing to your satisfaction, it will not be for the want of respects to you. And if anything turns up uncommon you shall all hear about it, so don't you and the rest of them not to think I don't think enough of them to write, for if you do you will be mistaken.*

By February 20th, preparations began in earnest as the Federal troops moved ever closer up the Peninsula. Eli described the activity in his camp:

*We are very badly confused at this time on account of the War matters. We are now ready and looking every hour for orders to leave. We received orders day before yesterday to cook four days rations and be ready to march. The wagons was sent off to Yorktown for crackers. We had no flour hardly but got plenty of sea crackers. We are expecting an attack every hour. The Yankeys is trying to flank us on water by sending a force up the York and James River and get in the rear of our army and if they try it with a sufficient force they may succeed but*

63

they need not to try it with less than fifty thousand men for we are well fortified all over the Peninsula. We have got hundreds of acres of land cut down between here and the Yankeys to blockade the way with trees so that they can't come on us with their artillery and it is most impossible for them to advance by land. Well, we receive bad news most every day lately. I suppose you have all heard of the fight at Roanoak Island, North Carolina. The enemy is in possession of it now. They killed many of our men and took two thousand prisoners. McMullins Regiment, that one that you all saw pass Mr.McInnis', is all taken prisoners but three companies. The Independent Blues is all in prison. They was taken at the Island fight. It is reported that they are now at Fortress Monroe about 20 miles from us but poor fellows we can't help them for all we are close by them. All our boys seems to sympathize a great deal for them but we see how it is. The

*Yankeys is getting the ends on us most everywhere they attack us. The dispatch of yesterday says that they have taken Fort Donelson in Tennessee and taken a great many of our men prisoners and that the citizens of Nashville had surrendered to the Yankeys but I hope to God it ain't the truth for if it is you may all look soon in Georgia for they will then have the main railroad and can run their forces both east and west. There was a great talk of peace when I first got to camp but oh to our sorrow we now see it was entirely a mistake. But there is one thing certain, we will hold them uneasy a long time before we will give it up. We will yield to none of their propositions without they be moved on our own terms. We will yield to death first. All our disasters do not seem to discourage our boys much. It seems to put a spirit of fight in them and I hope it will ever reign in them. We need not to think to end such a*

*war without some disastrous defeat for we need not to expect to always succeed but I hope in the long run that we may have peace and harmony again and that we may once more have the pleasure of tramping over the old hills that we have so often roamed and not only that but to have the pleasure of our friends and relations as an independent and free People. Let this situation not discourage us but let us endeavor to surmount all those gloomy scenes and show to the world that we are an Independent Nation!*

There was no more correspondence from Eli during the month of February. This absence of letters might have been due to the poor mail delivery at this time. Cobb noted that it sometimes took three weeks to get letters; moreover, very few newspapers were available to them. The Federals were threatening to take Suffolk, which was an important link to the Wilmington-Weldon Railroad. This railroad provided Lee's men with supplies and food, so holding the city became an important part of the Confederate defense plan. During the winter of 1861-1862 two of General Magruder's brigades were ordered to Suffolk. One of these brigades was that of Brigadier General George W. Randolph, and the other, Cobb's Second Brigade, which consisted of the 16th Ga.Regiment, the Georgia Legion, the 24th Georgia Regiment, the 15th North Carolina Regiment, and the 2nd Louisiana Regiment; a total of five thousand men. Abandoning their comfortable quarters at Yorktown, they headed south and arrived by train in Suffolk on March 7th. Here they found plenty to eat; shad, sweet potatoes, eggs, and peanuts, which helped compensate for the poor living quarters. Eli's letter of March 15th described the situation there:

*My Dear Mother,*
*I this morning take pleasure in writing you a few lines to let you know how we are getting on. As for myself I can't tell the truth and say that I am well but I think that it is the cold and being exposed to the weather and the broken rest waiting on the rest of the sick. I am sorry to tell such news to you but I reckon I had better tell the truth. All of my mess is down sick*

*but me. E.M. McDaniel has been very bad off for several days but I think he is some better this morning. W.N. Franklin had a hard chill this morning and is now bad off and also W.M. Mayfield had a chill this morning and is now very sick. A.W. has not come back from the hospital yet. He is in Williamsburg though I heard from him. He is improving so that takes all in my tent. There is a great deal of sickness in camp now but no more than I expected for we was the worst exposed of any set of men I ever saw but I hope that I will stay up to wait on the rest of them for they are not able to wait on each other but I fear that I will fail for I can hardly keep up now and have to be up and down all night. If I have to wait on them and drill too, I think that they ought to excuse me from all other duty but they will not do it but I will do the best I can for them but the best is bad enough for we are right where there is no accommodation to be found. They are in the tent lying on the ground but that is soldiers' fare anyhow. I can't write as I wish to for the poor boys is moaning with their pain so bitterly that it has confused my mind till I can't compose it but you need not to expect to derive much pleasure from this letter for there is no good news in it. We are expecting to leave here in a short time and if we do I don't know what in the world we will do with the sick for there is no hospital in Suffolk. But I reckon if we do leave they will be sent to Petersburg. It is now raining and a prospect for a wet spell and if there is one surely some of our sick will die. It looks hard that men should suffer so on account of the infamous Yankeys! Goodby My Dear Mother.*

In spite of the large number of sick, in less than two weeks, the troops had to continue moving south toward Goldsboro, North Carolina, to protect two important railroads. One ran south from Richmond to New Bern and Morehead City and the other from Wilmington to Weldon. Eli wrote a brief letter to his mother stating that all the sick were left in Suffolk and that he was the only one in his mess that was fit for battle.

They passed through Kinston, North Carolina, and on March 22nd they arrived in Goldsboro. They set up camp and named it Camp Randolph in honor of George Randolph, Secretary of War. The Federal forces had already taken New Bern and had begun moving toward Goldsboro. It was very crucial that the Confederates hold them back because it was felt that North Carolina would be devastated if they succeeded there. Within a week, twenty thousand men had gathered in the vicinity of Goldsboro. Eli described the situation in North Carolina to his mother in his letter of March 25th:

> *My Dear Mother,*
> *I am again permitted to drop you a few lines which is a great pleasure to me. We are four miles from Goldsboro, NC. We got here on the 24th of the month. I don't know what to write first for I have no good news to relate more than we are about 300 miles nearer home than we was at Yorktown though we are 500 miles from home yet. There is a great number of soldiers round here now. We are expecting a general engagement now every day. We got orders to hold ourselves in readiness to be ready at any minute. No person is allowed to leave the camp only to the spring and back but there is no telling what will be the result. But if the enemy still keeps advancing the result will be blood no doubt. The enemy is in possession of New Bern and are now eight miles toward Goldsboro and if they should succeed in getting this place they will soon ruin North Carolina. But we feel assured that we have the boys now who will stand the test and by so doing I hope that we can badly defeat them in their attempt. I hate to have to tell you that we had to witness the death of one of our worthiest soldiers last night named William Dickison. He died at 4 o'clock. We all mourn the loss of him very much, but there is one thing that I am glad to say, he died in Triumph of Honor. Throughout the company he will ever bear the name of a worthy soldier. I don't think he had an enemy in the company but poor fellow has passed through into a world unknown to mortality as many others has and may soon well follow. But I hope that if I be one that I will depart with honor to my Soul and Body as a good soldier. It makes me feel bad to see so many of our men dying. It looks like that our regiment has had hard luck but we had no reason to wonder. We will send William's corpse home by a man by the name of Odom that was here to see Andy and*

*"If you on earth I never see,*
*In all your prayers remember me."*
June, 1862

68

*Henry Odom. I remain your son as ever.*

Their stay in North Carolina was a short one. The Federals were driven away from Goldsboro, and Cobb's men were ordered to return to the Peninsula in April. They returned to Virginia on the Wilmington-Weldon Railroad. Catherine Edmondston, of Halifax County, noted in her diary that she saw the Sixteenth Georgia boys on the road between Petersburg and Weldon. She stated that they filled five long trains loaded with soldiers and much equipment. She specifically mentioned seeing Cobb's Legion and said that the men on the open cars were "most picturesquely huddled, some in groups, some singly, under any temporary shelter they could rig up, whether it be the corner of a tent or the body of a baggage wagon." She thought the diversity of their baggage and its arrangement would have made a good subject for an artist to

*"I write this with my own hand to testify that I am yet in the land of the living and all honor and glory be to God for his care over me."*
May, 1863

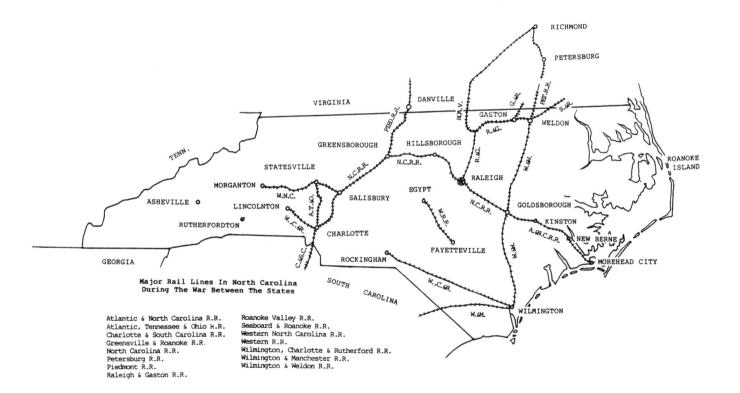

Major Rail Lines In North Carolina
During The War Between The States

Atlantic & North Carolina R.R.
Atlantic, Tennessee & Ohio R.R.
Charlotte & South Carolina R.R.
Greensville & Roanoke R.R.
North Carolina R.R.
Petersburg R.R.
Piedmont R.R.
Raleigh & Gaston R.R.

Roanoke Valley R.R.
Seaboard & Roanoke R.R.
Western North Carolina R.R.
Western R.R.
Wilmington, Charlotte & Rutherford R.R.
Wilmington & Manchester R.R.
Wilmington & Weldon R.R.

paint. She noted seeing cooking utensils, camp furniture, trunks, muskets, stools, wagons, cannon, tents, caissons, beds, blankets, wheels, and men all thrown together at random. She said they were very anxious for news and eagerly held out their hands for the morning papers which were brought from Richmond.

In early April, General George McClellan landed in Virginia with a large force of Federal troops at the tip of the Peninsula, which jutted out into Hampton Roads, with the York River on one side and the Chickahominy River on the other. McClellan's aim was to move up the Peninsula and take control of Richmond.

This was the first phase of Union strategy to defeat the South. It was believed that taking the Confederate capital would end the war very quickly. It has been estimated that McClellan landed with eighty to one hundred thousand troops. Magruder stationed his men all the way from Yorktown southward to the James River.

*"Ma, you ought to be here to eat Irish Potatoe Pie with me and EM and AW. We can make as nice a chicken pie out of potatoes as you ever saw. We make them in a skillet and put butter and pepper in them and they are good a plenty for an old dirty soldier."*
*July, 1862*

Just south of Yorktown was the Warwick River, which ran through a thick woods and swamp. This river flowed southward across the Peninsula into the James River on which were located four dams. Two of them had been built some years prior to this for water power for two gristmills, Wynn's and Lee's Mills. Between these two dams, Magruder built two more dams which would permit him to back up the water over the low-lying country making any advancement by the enemy very difficult.

Eli wrote his mother on April 16th and in his letter he indicated that they would probably have a fight that day, which they did. The three hour battle left twenty killed and seventy wounded in the sixteenth regiment:

*Dear Mother,*
*In great haste I will write you a few lines this morning to let you know that I am well. The soldiers are coming in as fast as the boats can bring them. There will be one hundred and fifty thousand men here by night. I think they are fixing for it now every day but I can't tell when it will be. It may be before night and it may not be in a week. Do the best you can and write soon.*

70

It must have been just after Eli finished his letter that his regiment was moved into position on the west side of the Warwick River at Dam No. 1. This dam was halfway between Wynn's Mill and Lee's Mill and was considered to be the most vulnerable place in the line of defense. Early on the morning of the 16th, the Federals made a furious attack on the Confederate troops, bombarding the woods with mortar shells from six artillery pieces and with an entire regiment of sharpshooters pressing them back. By afternoon, several companies of Vermont troops had crossed the river just below the dam and had taken over some of the Confederate trenches. The situation looked hopeless for a while, but General Cobb went among his troops giving them encouragement, and by afternoon his men rallied and forced the Yankees back across the river. The Federals lost an estimated six hundred men while the Confederates lost only seventy five. This battle, known as the Battle of Lee's Mill, was significant because it was the first assault made on an entrenched position by the Federals forces.

The day before the battle started it had rained so much that the trenches were filled with water and for more than two weeks after the battle had been fought, Cobb's men were standing in knee-deep mud with no tents to cover them. Since the enemy kept firing at them day and night, fires were forbidden so that the enemy could not see them in the dark. The men were also in constant danger from Union gunboats firing on them from the York River. Eli's letters of April 23rd and 25th describe their ordeal:

*My Dearest Mother*
*I am again permitted to answer another letter from you which came to hand yesterday which gave me great pleasure to hear you was all well for that is a little more than I can say for myself at present. I have been rather puny for several days but I have not been past doing duty but if I don't get better I will have to report to the doctor. But I reckon that it is cold that's the matter with me. Being so exposed to the weather and broke of my rest for we ain't got to sleep but two nights since the 16th, the day of the fight. Now I am going to tell something about the fight*

*"I am away off from camp about a half a mile in an old outhouse upstairs by myself a-studying about old times. I have seen more pleasure today than I have in a week for I am tired being with so many men. A person has to slip off if he ever gets to himself."*
Undated.

71

but I know that there will be so many different descriptions given. I hate to say anything about it but I aim to tell the truth if I can. Well on the 16th about 3:00 in the evening, the enemy made their attack and run into our pickets. We was about half a mile from the line when the firing commenced. We all went in double quick to the rescue of our brothers and when we got there the enemy was nearly to our breastworks, in fact they had part of them in possession and we run in an open fire on them. We did not have time to organize our regiment. We all run in and shot when we had the chance and never formed no line. If a man could get behind a tree it was alright. Some of the boys never fired a gun. Some lay behind logs as close to the ground as young rabbits till the battle was over. One or two of our company run back to camp but as for my part I thought I would stay till the fun was over. There was the 7th, 8th, 11th, and 16th Georgia Regiments engaged in the fight, along with the 5th North Carolina and a Louisiana Regiment. The Yankees made the North Carolina regiment retreat from their own breast-works and the Yanks took it but in come our 7th Georgia brothers and their colonel immediately ordered a charge and the brave boys obeyed the command with the greatest applause and hollering and retook the battery without the loss of a man with one or two wounded. The fight lasted till about dark when the enemy retired. Our boys killed and wounded about eighty but we don't know the exact number. We fought mostly across a pond that Jim Magruder had made on a small creek. But the brave rascals made a charge through the pond on us but there was but few of them that lived to get back to the side where they started. There was only two of our regiment killed and six or seven wounded. Old Mr. Gasaway was killed dead and one of Captain Sketton's men was killed. I was standing in two feet of him when he was shot. Me and him was shooting from behind the same tree. I think the old fellow killed two of them before they got him. Me and him was before any of our company. We saw in about seventy five yards of them and I took two fair pops at them from that tree but there was so much smoke I could not see whether I killed anyone or not but I don't know what is the reason for I took a deliberate aim at them. The old man was shot right in the forehead. It did not frighten me

Old Mr. Gassaway was the first man in Ely's company to be killed in action.

72

*as bad as I expected it would but I tell you when the bullets would whistle around my head I felt sort of ticklish. But I thought that there was no use in standing back. If I got killed I couldn't help it but as the good Father would have it, I came out without a scratch. That was on the 16th and we had to stand picket till the 20th without any relief and I tell you it has most outdone me. We will have to go out again tomorrow. We haven't had no attack since the 16th. Only the other night there was a few of them running into our pickets but they didn't follow them back to our regiment. The pickets was afraid to go out anymore.*

*Dear Mother,*
*I will write only a few lines though cause I hain't time to write much. This leaves me well as to health but I feel very much wearied as I have just come off of picket duty. This morning we had some heavy skirmishing but none killed on our side. One was wounded in the face. N.B. you told me to do my best at the Yanks. You needn't to doubt but what I looked low down in the sights at them and I think that I injured two of them. We are expecting another fight everyday but I can't tell nothing about it. I have been in service nearly nine months and I have never saw such times as we have now for a man is in danger of his life to leave the camp and the orders that was give to pickets that relieved us this morning was that if any man run or give orders to run without orders from the Commanding Officer he is to be shot. There was a large force come on us this morning and I tell you the bullets sung round our heads like mad bees but they soon retired and the firing is now ceased. There is about thirty regiments of Georgians here now. We miss old man Gassaway mightly but the poor old fellow is lying over here in the woods and his brains is scattered over the ground. I was in three feet of him when he got killed. As Bill Dyer says, some of the boys leaped to the rear but I will mention no names and tell no tales out of school. So I will close with my best wishes.*

After this confrontation with the Federal forces, General Bryan commended the Sixteenth for the gallantry displayed by

both officers and men.

General McClellan actually came within sight of the church spires of Richmond before turning back. Even though Lincoln considered him a failure and later relieved him of command, he came closer to the Confederate capital than any other Union officer until the end of the war. On May 3rd, General Joseph Johnston ordered the troops to move off the Peninsula and Cobb's Legion retreated to Richmond. By May 13th they were four miles from Richmond below the Mechanicsville Bridge on the southern bank of the Chickahominy River, where they began to prepare for the defense of the city.

On May 29th, Eli wrote about expecting a general engagement with the Yankees at any moment. He said:

> *We have moved since I wrote to you last. We moved off of the river on the other side of Richmond. We are in about three miles of Richmond but I can't get no chance to go to see my old friends. There is great fear of the Yankeys taking Richmond. They are in sight of us with a large force. We are expecting a general engagement every day. It is thought there will be the hardest fighting around this place that ever has been heard of for the enemy will do their game fighting to get the city but our men has formed a resolution for the streets to flow with blood before we give it up. There was fighting in hearing of us on the 27th. We could hear their guns plain but we have not heard how it went.*

Two days after this letter was written, General Johnston attacked the Federals at Seven Pines, a few miles southeast of Richmond. Cobb's Brigade did not get into the action, however, and remained in their camp with orders to clean up the battle sites, burying the dead and removing any offensive matter. Eli wrote to his mother from this camp, which was probably near Mechanicsville, a village, five miles from Richmond. The battle was fought there June 26th.

> *My Dear Mother and Sisters,*
> *I seat myself this morning to inform you that I am well but feel very drowsy for I have just got up and it is about two hours by sun. We have had but very little fighting here since the 31st but we had some very heavy skirmishing. One of our regiment attacked the Yankeys the other evening and they fired in like*

*smoke. For a while I thought that we was going to have a general engagement. Our regiment was called in line of battle and all prospects for a fight was shown but the Yankeys run back and our men never followed them. We are looking for another big fight everyday but we can't tell when. We are camped in burning distance of each other. We bum each other's camps every day. The Yankees threw a bum in the camp of the 8th Georgia Regiment yesterday and killed one man and wounded four others. It is thought that they will die. One of their legs was shot all to pieces and another one's shoulder was shot off. There is some killed or wounded everyday on picket. A man never knows what time he may be shot but we have not lost narry man yet but the 24th Georgia has lost two or three. They was on picket the other day and we sent a scouting party out over the lines to stir up the Yanks and the password was "Stonewall" so if they had to run back that our pickets would know them. One of the pickets was a man in front of his line and he hollowed "Stonewall" to him but it happened to be a Yank and in the place of giving the password in return he shot him through and says, "Goddam you that is Stonewall!" But another one of our pickets immediately shot the Yank. I guess that he thought he had hit a Stonewall! I don't like this place for a camp. It is a low level place and no good water. We use water out of a little hole dug out in the ground about three feet deep and you know that it ain't good but I expect we will have to stay here a good while but I don't care for we are all in for the war anyhow. I would be glad if I could camp somewhere on Beaver Run. There is so many of the invading scamps round us we must not choose our place to live if we intend to be a free people. It grieves me to lie round here in the shade knowing how hard you all have to work at home but these things we can't help. I hear the cannons a shooting now. They will keep it up all day but none of their shot don't reach our regiment. So with my respects and well wishes I will close for this time hoping to hear from you soon.*

Eli didn't realize as he wrote this letter that the Seven Days' Battle was about to begin. Several days prior to the battle, Cobb's men had been entrenched in an area known as "Burnt

Chimney" on the Nine Mile Road. On June 26th, the Sixteenth Regiment along with thousands of other Confederate soldiers crossed the Chickahominy River moving into Mechanicsville, where they took the town. When they reached Beaver Dam Creek however, the Federals were heavily fortified, and they shattered the Georgia lines. Over three hundred Georgians died that day in the swamp. They pushed the Union troops on, however, with battles at Gaines Mill, Savage Station, and Frasier's Farm. McClellan led his troops away from the area seeking refuge with his reinforcements on Malvern Hill. Cobb's Georgians pursued him on June 30th and July lst. He left Burnt Chimney with twenty seven hundred men, and as a result of the prolonged march without food or rest, only about fifteen hundred of them were able to fight when they reached Crew's Farm on July lst. Eli wrote his mother a letter from there on July 6th which described the situation:

> *Affectionate Mother,*
> *I am once more permitted to write you a few lines to let you know that I am yet alive and well but that is more than many of my friends can say and I know that it is for nothing good that I've done that I am spared but a great Blessing bestowed upon me. But the God of all nations has for some purpose brought me through another engagement unhurt and I feel thankful to say so for while many of my brother soldiers were slain on the field. We had been pursuing the Yankeys for three days. We pursued them hot all day Sunday when in the evening we came up with them which terminated in a hard fight. But our regiment was not engaged in it. We stayed there all night and next morning we started out after them again. We marched all day Monday when in the evening another struggle insued lasting from 5 o'clock till 9 o'clock with unmerciful fighting. Our regiment got there just as the battle was over. We stayed on the battlefield that night. Our line was formed over many dead and wounded Yankeys. We eat breakfast over all their dead, some with their brains out on the ground. After eating we formed a line of battle and started out throught the woods on another Yankey drive. We marched till about 12 o'clock when news come to us that General Jackson was before us with*

*thirty thousand men after the Yanks. Then we turned our course and in the evening we came up with the Yankeys in line of battle in a noble position with a heavy battery in good range of us. We made an immediate attack and with large forces on both sides. But they having all advantages of the ground and our men not expecting them so close by that our men was not properly organized for the engagement but we had run on them and we was obliged to fight or retreat. The first command given was to fix bayonets and charge the battery which the gallant men in great heroism did but we had to charge through an open field for about a half mile under the open and well directed fire of a heavy battery well supported with infantry. The grapeshot and bums cut our lines down so rapidly our officers finding it could not be taken. We was ordered back for form and tried it again but did not succeed and retired the second time. It is amazing at that range how any of us got through to tell the fate of others for bumbshells was flying round as thick as a hailstorm. Great destruction on both sides but the number is not yet ascertained. There was several of our regiment killed and a good many wounded but none of our company was killed. D.W.Haney was wounded in the knee. The doctor says that he will lose his leg. Mallock was shocked with the bursting of a bum in his face injuring his eyes. Two of our captains got wounded and one of them is now dead. A piece of bum scalped me on the side of the head making a mark but not breaking the skin. It burnt so I thought I was really wounded. Next morning I went over the battlefield and it was awful to look at the scene of destruction that had been done. The field was lying thick with the noble Southerners being trampled on.*

Eli was describing the events of June 30th when Cobb's Brigade moved up the slopes of Malvern Hill. They were driven back several times with a great loss of life. Of the men who charged the batteries on Malvern Hill, one third were killed or wounded. Later the Confederates were successful in taking the hill. McClellan and his troops had gotten away, but only after thousands on both sides had been killed. This battle

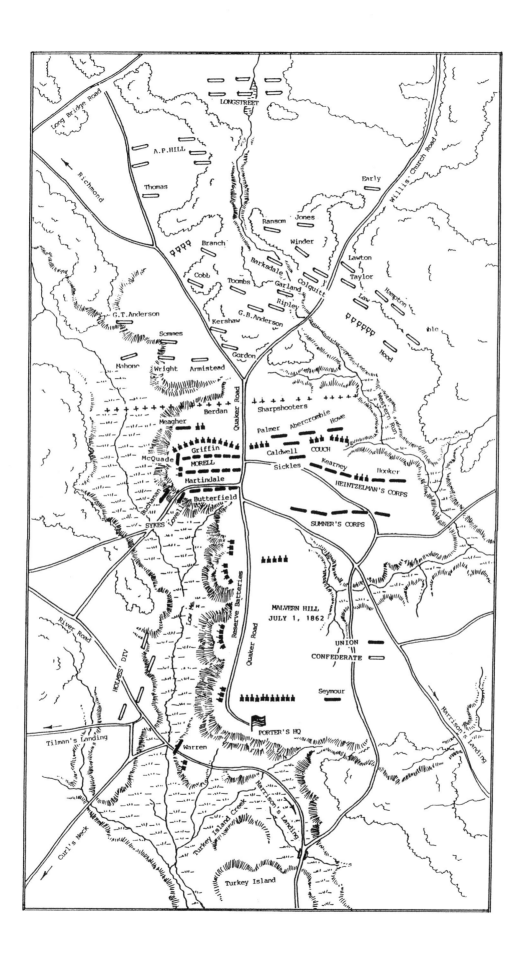

was the last of the Seven Days Battle, and Richmond was still in Confederate hands. By this time, Eli had seen more suffering and dying than he had ever before experienced in his life. In a letter he wrote to Caroline a few weeks later, he began writing more nostagically about home than ever before:

> *I have saw the wounded hauled off in horse wagons, just thrown in like hogs, some with their legs off and some with their arms off and in terrible condition. It would have been a great pleasure to go to general meeting with you and Mamma. I can turn back to the past times when I was at my old Native and happy home and think of the many enjoyments that was there. It is a pleasure to think of it yet, but it is as you said. I fear that I will never have the pleasure of roaming my Native Country again. But I will live in hopes and if I do not despair then it is not impossible.*

By the end of the month, Eli's regiment had moved. He described his new site as "a beautiful campground with plenty of the best kind of water." He told his mother, "Don't be uneasy about me for the life of a soldier just suits me, but I had rather be at home to get some of them big apples growing before the door."

After the intense fighting on the Peninsula, General Cobb was physically sick. He was also discouraged with the tremendous loss of life among the men under his command, and he requested permission to go home to Georgia to regain his health. Since Cobb had had previous experience in prisoner exchange General Lee requested that before leaving he take charge of helping facilitate the exchange of the thousands of prisoners that had been taken in the battles on the Peninsula.

The Confederacy had no way to accommodate so many men and had to find some way to care for them. Cobb attempted to carry out his orders, but he was too ill to do so and was taken home to recuperate. The number of prisoners taken grew even greater as the weeks passed, and in a letter dated July 20th, near Richmond, Eli wrote, "I have not heard from our wounded boys, only that all that was able was parolled and sent to Richmond. I don't know who was able, and as for those who was taken and not hurt. We don't know anything about them though I suppose they were sent to Washington."

General Cobb was given a thirty day furlough in July and returned in August to his regiment, then camped near the James River about ten miles below Richmond. In the coming days his new-found strength would be sorely tested, as would that of the men of the Sixteenth Georgia as they moved into Union territory.

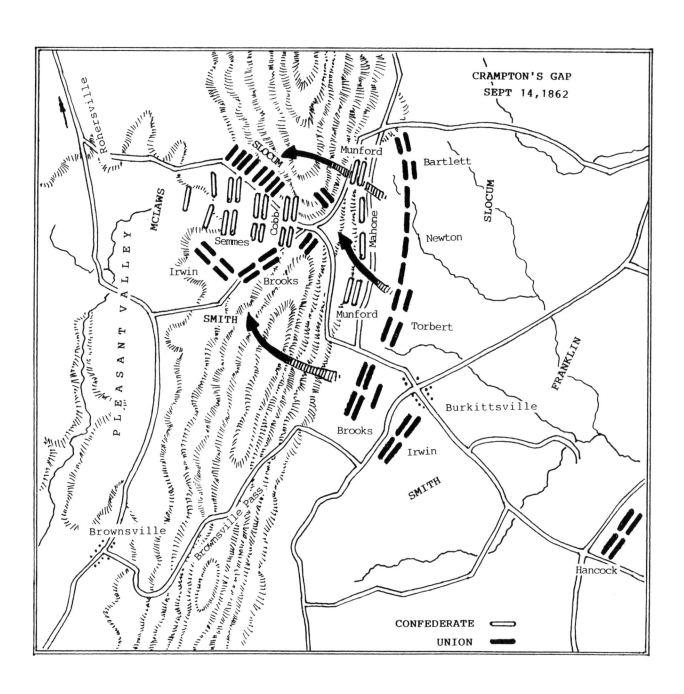

## *Chapter IV*
## *The Maryland Invasion*

IN AUGUST COBB'S BRIGADE became a part of McLaw's division with orders to move north and join Lee's Army of Northern Virginia. They were loaded on railroad cars in Richmond with their horses and equipment and taken to a place near Hanover Junction where they joined up with twelve thousand other Confederate soldiers. Orders were received to move out from camp, and the men were ordered to prepare three days of rations.

Under the command of Major General D.H. Hill, they marched to Rapidan Station, covering 60 miles in a three day period. They crossed two mountain ranges and the Potomac River before reaching their destination. Cobb was furious with Hill for what he called an inhumane march and complained bitterly about the condition in which it left his men. Many of the mendied from heat exhaustion along the road and hundreds more had sore feet and had to be left along the way. The Georgia Legion started out with five hundred men and arrived at Rapidan Station with only three hundred and thirteen.

On August 30th, Cobb's Brigade kept moving north from Rapidan Station to Leesburg, Virginia. In early September, they crossed the battlefield on which the second Battle of Manassas had been fought a few days prior to this, and saw the horrible evidence of the battle. Eli described the sight in his letter of September 25th:

> *I passed the Manassas battleground and I saw hundreds of dead Yanks. They had lay on the field till they was as black as a Negro with their eyes and tongues swelled out of their head.*

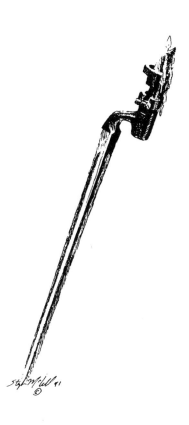

This scene gave the men false hope however, for they thought the Yankees would surely give up soon. But as they would find out, it would not be so easy. Moving northward, the Georgians waded across the Potomac River on September 6th and reached Frederick, Maryland on September 9th. Lee wanted to take the war into the North by way of Maryland for several reasons. He knew that many people in Maryland were sympathetic to the South, and felt that if they saw the Southern army on their soil, it would give them the courage to support the Confederates. He also felt that the movement north would draw the Federals' attention from Richmond, giving the Confederates a chance to strengthen their defense of the city.

Probably his most important reason for this movement northward was to protect his source of food, the Shenandoah Valley, and prevent it from being taken by the Federals. The people there, however, were hostile to the Southern troops, even closing their shops to keep them from getting needed supplies. It was at this point that Lee decided to split his army, with one part moving to Hagerstown, and the other part to Union-held Harper's Ferry. Between these two places lay South Mountain. Crampton's Gap, one of the passes through the mountain would be the site of the Georgians next confrontation with the Union army , and would be one of the bloodiest fights they would encounter.

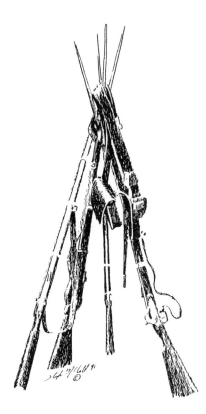

Cobb's Regiment was ordered by General McLaws to close Crampton's Gap and hold it "if it cost the life of every man in his regiment," which it very nearly did. The regiment moved up to the top of South Mountain without much opposition, but after reaching the top, they saw some of the other regiments having a difficult time with the Union troops, so some of the regiments went down to help them. Suddenly, the center of the line began to cave in and the men panicked, running down the western slope of South Mountain, "like a flock of frightened sheep." Apparently someone in the regiment went back to Gwinnett County and told Eli's family that he had run from the fight at South Mountain. In a letter to his mother, Eli expressed his anger about this accusation, but does not name his accuser:

*I heard that he said that I was not in the fight at South Mountain and that I run before I got into it and that I never had been in narry fight and all such tales that would degrade an honorable soldier. We know the way to find whether those words is well to rely upon is to ask the officers that has been in command of me all the time and see what they say about it. I think they will all say that I have always been found at my post. The rest of the boys that is there on furlough I think will certify the same. I have always tried to discharge my duty in the service of my country as a soldier and for him to talk about me in that way it hurts my feelings very much. He has never been in but one fight but if he don't give me satisfaction when he comes back I think he will be in another one! I intend to have satisfaction either by words or deeds. I reckon I have said enough about that for I think more than I say.*

Some of the men reported the affair differently, saying that Cobb ran them down right into the Yankee lines and then ordered them to retreat when he saw that they were in trouble. They said that when they couldn't retreat in an orderly manner, that they "had to crawl down the mountain with the Yankees shooting them like squirrels."

The Second Brigade, of which the Sixteenth Regiment was a part, lost between three hundred and five hundred men that day. It was estimated that the Confederates were greatly outnumbered, having only twenty two hundred men as opposed to fifteen thousand Union troops. Cobb's Georgians went into the battle with two hundred and fifty men and returned with only eighty three. Judging by this battle, Cobb must have been a better politician than a strategist. Even though Cobb's Brigade had received terrible punishment at South Mountain, Stonewall Jackson's regiment was able to take Harper's Ferry from the Federals while the men of the Sixteenth were engaged in the battle. This battle had also slowed the Union forces down, giving Lee time to get Jackson back to assist him in the drive into Maryland. All of this activity was setting the stage for the big battle at Antietam.

On September 20th, after the battle at Crampton's Gap, Cobb went back across the Potomac River to a place near Martinsburg, Virginia to await further orders to move back southward. Eli wrote to his mother from Martinsburg on September 25th describing their recent ordeal at Crampton's Gap:

*My Dear Respected Mother,*
*After a long time of silence I am again permitted to write you a few lines to let you know that my respects still remain with you. I am enjoying good health at this time. That is a great blessing. I have nothing of a cherring nature to write. Since I wrote you last I have had some rough times marching from Richmond. We are about two hundred miles from Richmond and I think that we have marched three hundred miles to get here. We marched thirteen days in succession and have been marching nearly every day since we went over into Maryland to see how their pulse beat. We stayed about two weeks with*

*a heavy loss. We gained a great victory at Harper's Ferry. There was twelve thousand Yankees that surrendered there without attempting to fight their way out. They tried their dearest to get reinforcements and if we had held back four hours longer they would reached them. The surrender was made on Monday morning at 8 o'clock. The evening before General McClellan advanced with a large army to help his friends at the Ferry. We then had to almost double quick about five miles to meet them and when we got there our force was too weak to stand our hand with them. Now I can't say no more till I tell you the bad news. There was about two thirds of our Brigade killed, wounded, or taken prisoner. We went into the fight with thirty men in our company and lost eighteen of them though we cant tell who was killed for it was every man for himself. For they fell back on our right and let the enemy flank us. They come in near taking all of our regiment prisoners. There was one time I thought it impossible for me to escape for I was entirely exhausted with heat and the Yankeys right after us and the bullets flying round me like hail. I will now give the names of the missing. First Captain Reeder was wounded and left on the field.*[Note: He was shot through the thigh, captured, and taken to the US Hospital at Burkittsville, Maryland. His leg was amputated and he died September 24th.] *W.T. Mason was wounded in the beginning of the fight. He was shot in the hip and there was no chance to get him off the field for we had to retreat in great haste.* [Note: He died at US Hospital at Burkittsville November 27th.] *Ben Matthews was wounded and left on the field also.* [Note: Died of wounds at Burkittsville September 14th.] *George Jackson was shot in the leg.* [Note: He died of wounds at Burkittsville October 16th]. *E.M. fell on the retreat and some say he was only overcome with the heat. He is either shot or taken prisoner* [Note: E.M. McDaniel, Eli's cousin was not taken prisoner until sometime in 1863.] *We have all reasons to believe that A.W. was killed.* [Note; A.W. McDaniel, another of Eli's cousins was captured at Crampton's Gap September 14th and died later.] *Also missing was J.R. Scott, J.R. Davis, G.W. Flowers, Linsy Smith, Green Hamby, John Long, John Peden, Luit Martin,*

*Samp Garner, and T.M. Gazaway. That is all I can account for. We suppose the rest was taken.* {Ed. note: Of all these missing men, all were accounted for except Green Hamby, who was killed at Crampton's Pass on September 14th.}*I feel perfectly lost since the fight for my mess was all killed or wounded that was along but me. It made me feel awful to think that they was all in the hands of the enemy but I could not redeem them with sympathy for I come very near being with them. I stopped once to give up for I nearly give out but the nearer the Yanks come the worse I was scared so I tried it again. It was about dark and what few of us got away got scattered very bad. I traveled till 10 o'clock in the night to get back down to our old station and I got lost but I found an old outhouse and stayed till morning when I found the regiment. There was only seventy five men left in it,seven in our company. We lay in line of battle till the next morning and the news came that Harper's Ferry had surrendered and all the cheering you never heard. Then we marched all day and all night on Tuesday. We waded the Potomac River about day on Wednesday morning and with our little squad went into another hard fight. We only had five men in our company. The fight lasted from daylight till dark and we saw some of the hardest fighting that has been. I never saw the like of wounded men in my life, but none of our company was lost in that fight. We lost all of our knapsacks and blankets. We have to lie round the fire of night. If I had time, I could write a long time but I must hasten for it is most time for our inspection. We are expecting another fight everyday. I think if this army don't get some rest that the men will all die. We have been marching all day over the mountains and stop at night and start again by day. But I have had good health all the time.*

*You wanted to know if I needed any clothes. If you can get them I would be glad of a good suit of jeans for we are run about so much we can't keep nothing only what we have on our backs and one good suit would last me nearly all winter. Today my mind is so confused that I can't write as I would wish to. I hate to send such news for I know that it will hurt many feelings, but you must not take it to heart too much for it can't be hoped. We can only hope that the Yanks may treat the ones they captured kindly and that they may return yet. I have went through many close places since I wrote you last. Perhaps the next close place I will not come through and if this be the last time you ever hear from me I want you to remember that it was God's will for me to go that way which none can hinder so with my love to you all I will close. Goodby my good old Mother if I never see you again.*

It was reported that after this battle, many of the Southern troops were sick, malnourished, and exhausted. Most of them were also barefoot by this time, and in only a few weeks, Eli changed his mind about his Mother sending him more clothes:

*If you get a good chance to send me any clothes I will pay the man that brings them for his trouble. If you don't have a good opportunity I will try to make out without them though I am like a tarapan. All I have got is on my back and that is dirty and common but I am as well fixed as the most of the boys. I lost my blanket in the fight of the 17th and lay out on the ground till the other day when I bought me a blanket and a small tent which cost me $5.00.*

In this same letter, he described his feelings after having survived the terrible carnage at Crampton's Gap:

*My mess has decreased for the last three months. Out of ten they are all sick, killed, or wounded but oh what can it be but kind providence that I am not hurt. I sometimes look back and feel indebted to thank my God for his goodness to me and to preserve me while so many as worthy as I have fell by my side. I have come through four engagements without a scratch but perhaps on the fifth one I may fall in the field but that is the risk to run. I would be glad if they could settle this affair without anymore blood for there undoubtedly has ever been more blood shed in this war than has ever been recorded before. But it is the opinion of the most of the men that there will be hard fighting yet.*

The hard fighting yet to come would be at a place called Fredericksburg.

*"We drew 2 months wages the other day. We are paid up to the first of March but I will have to keep it for I was nearly out of money for I had to spend some on my teeth. They was decaying so fast I thought I had better have them pluggesd and that cost me 15 dollars."*
Undated.

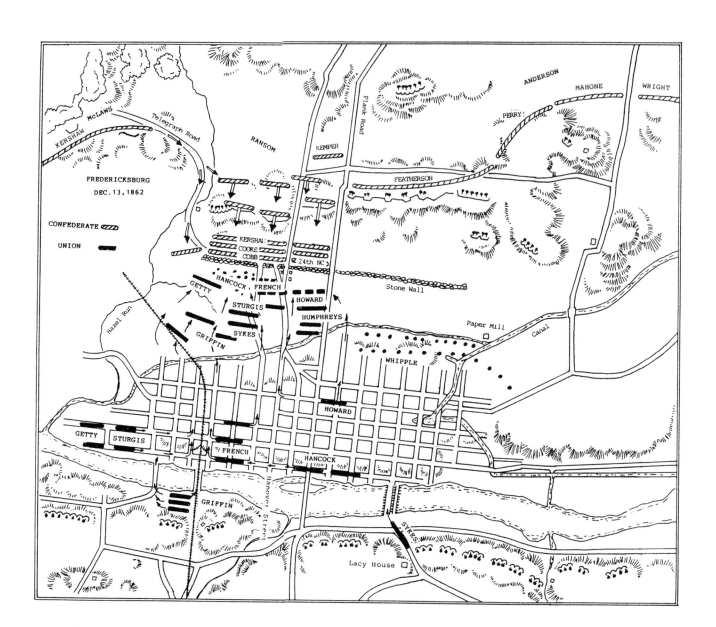

FREDERICKSBURG
DEC. 13, 1862

CONFEDERATE

UNION

McLAWS

KERSHAW

Telegraph Road

RANSOM

KEMPER

Plank Road

ANDERSON

PERRY

MAHONE

WRIGHT

FEATHERSON

KERSHAW
COOKE
COBB

24th NC

Stone Wall

GETTY

HANCOCK FRENCH

STURGIS

HOWARD

Hazel Run

GRIFFIN

SYKES

HUMPHREYS

Paper Mill

Canal

WHIPPLE

HOWARD

GETTY

STURGIS

FRENCH

HANCOCK

Hanover Street

GRIFFIN

SYKES

Lacy House

## Chapter V
## Behind the Stone Wall at Fredericksburg

After the battle of Antietam, Eli's company moved south to Fredericksburg, Virginia where in December they encountered Federal troops in a great battle. Fredericksburg is just sixty miles north of Richmond, so the Union objective in staging this battle was to make another attempt to capture the Confederate capital.

In setting up their defenses at Fredericksburg, McLaw's Division was stationed on the high ground behind the city with Anderson's regiment on his left, Pickett's regiment on his right, and Howell Cobb's brother, Thomas Cobb with his Brigade up on Marye's Heights. He strengthened his position by preparing rifle pits and laying a barricade of felled trees with the branches pointing outward. At the foot of his front line was a sunken road that was protected by a stone wall. He had a ditch dug on the lower side of the road with the dirt that was removed, banked in front of the wall to make trenches from which the artillery would have the advantage of point blank firing range. Howell Cobb's Georgians were positioned here, and he said they had the best position on the line. McLaws himself was given the job of guarding the riverfront.

The town was located on the Rappahannock River, so the Union forces had to devise some means of crossing it to get into the town. They began preparing for the crossing by constructing pontoon bridges at three places along the river. They worked under cover of night so the Confederate pickets couldn't see what they were doing. Since the ice was very thick in the river, it took them longer to build the bridges than they had planned and during this delay the Confederates were able to

prepare for the coming attack. They worked out a signal system to warn each other whenever the Yankees began moving across the river. The signal would be the firing of one gun followed quickly by a second cannon shot.

On November 21st, the local people were given the opportunity to leave before the firing commenced, since their houses would be in the direct line of fire between the two opposing forces. Many of them left when given the chance, but others decided to stay in their cellars. General Lee admired these courageous people who left their homes before the shelling began. He was touched by the "piteous sight of women and children turned out into the December cold and forced to wade in the mud." Eli also wrote home describing their exodus from the town:

> *Dear Mother,*
>
> *It is with pleasure that I write you a few lines to let you know that I am in tolerable health with the exception of a bad cold. We have no fighting here yet. The enemy left Culpepper and has concentrated a large force at this place. We are here very close together with the Rappahannock River between us. The Yankey camp is on one hill and us on the other in plain view. We have been looking for them to bumb us every day. They ordered the people to leave Fredericksburg the 21st by 9 o'clock. It was distressing to see the women and little children leaving their homes and all that they had left behind and taking the muddy road on foot. We could just meet them in droves. It is raining and very cold. Their poor little feet was as red as a dove's. The people did not have time to make their escape any other way but the enemy has not fired on the town yet They are fortifying on both sides. I would not be surprised if we did not spend the winter here.*

*"This war has brought many troubles on us but let us support it to the last. Let none flinch nor falter but stand steadfast and honorably in defense of our rights and out country will be hard to redeem and let everyone bear a part."*
Undated.

Finally the signal was heard to commence firing and the first target was the Union company that was building the pontoon bridge near Deep Run. The ice on the river was over a half inch thick and made the job of laying the bridge very difficult.

In spite of the Confederate sharpshooters picking them off, the bridge builders continued to work. When Burnside gave the order, one hundred and forty seven guns opened fire on the town. Hoping to drive the Confederates out,the Union Army only accomplished the destruction of many houses and streets. Confederate troops had taken cover in cellars of houses and ditches and were not hurt by this first assault. The Federals tried to continue their bridge building but were driven back again. After several more attempts, they were finally successful in getting across on December 12th, with the main attack coming on December 13th.

General Thomas Cobb's Georgians, along with a North Carolina regiment, rained down a devastating barrage of bullets on the Federal troops as they tried to come up the hill toward the Confederate forces. As new troops moved in to replace those who had fallen, they had to step over the dead and wounded. Longstreet described the Federals as falling "like the steady dripping of rain from the eaves of a house."

The Union lost nine thousand men that day, while the Confederates lost fewer than nineteen hundred. One of the greatest losses was that of Thomas Cobb, who fell on the sunken road. Some of the wounded were left on the frozen ground for as much as two days without getting any assistance and died from exposure. Many of the wounded, unable to move, were burned to death when the cannon fire ignited the dry grass. This horrible sight of comrades dying in agony must have been on Eli's mind when he wrote the following letter:

*It looks like that destruction is spread abroad in our land. So many of our friends dying and other calamities almost as bad, but we need not to expect anything better. I just believe that is the sin and pride of the people that brought it on and I believe the people will have to come more equinoxial before times ever gets any better and times is not half as bad now as they will be. I don't see any other chance only for us all to suffer for the want of common [illegible] if the war don't close soon and I see no prospect for that.*

By the end of this confrontation with the Yankees, Eli

*"There was 32 solgers the other day broke the ice and was baptised and old Preacher staid in the water till he baptized 22 of them."*
Undated.

had lost some of the optimism he had shown earlier in his military career and did not view the experience at Fredericksburg as a sweet victory. By December 15th, it was all over and Burnside's troops went back across the river. Fredericksburg was still in Southern hands.

Several explanations have been given for the Union defeat at Fredericksburg. One was the lack of good maps and the difficulty in obtaining accurate information about the Confederate troops' whereabouts. The scarcity of provisions also added to the Union forces' problems. Some analysts have suggested that Union failure in ending the war sooner was due to their trying to take control of isolated towns and areas like Fredericksburg rather than concentrating on destroying the Rebel army itself. The early months of 1863 were relatively quiet ones. Eli's letters contained no war news, but were filled with mundane things like the cost of replacing some of his worn out clothes and his desire to go home and see his mother:

*Fredericksburg, Va January 14th 1863*

*Dear Mother,*
*This morning I take pleasure in writing you a few lines though it seems like a difficult matter to hear from you. I am well this morning. I really hope this may find you all well. I have nothing new to write this morning but I thought that I would tell you that we had received that box of jeans and clothes that was started when I was at home. It come to the Co on the 12th. Some of the clothing was very badly damaged and almost rotten, but none of the individual things was injured. I drawed me another coat out of the box but I have to pay $7.50 for it to make those equal that don't get one But I had rather pay that for such coats than to draw the government clothes. I sold them leggings for two dollars. The regiment is about to draw money I think then I can pay for them. I will do the best I can with it. Mr. Raborn and Tom Todd is expecting to start home on a furlough in a day or two and if they get off I will send the money by them.*

*Behind the Stone Wall at Fredericksburg*

*Dear Mother*

*I hant got time to write you much. I am well this morning and I hope this will find you well but I fear it will not from the reading of the last letter you said for me to try to come home and see you. Dear Mother nothing in the world would afford me more pleasure than to do so but there is no chance to get off but if you don't improve in health before long I want you to let me know it and if there is any chance in the world to come I will come for I don't think that you will live long without you take better care of yourself and it would most kill me to never see you again. If you don't improve in health and desires me to visit you write a special letter to Captain Cain and one to me at the same time stating the case in it and I think the captain will do all he can to get me a special leave of absence. Ma you seem to be very uneasy about me for fear I suffer with the cold. I don't want you to think so for when we are at camp and not on picket or other duty we fare very well. We have got good tents and plenty straw to lie on and we lie very comfortable. My pillow feels good and soft to my jaws. I let John Wallis and Tom Matthews take it one night.*

As Spring arrived, restless troops became anxious to meet the enemy again and hopefully to finally resolve the conflict.

## Chapter VI

## Crossing the Dare Mark at Chancellorsville

AFTER THE BATTLE at Fredericksburg, the Union Army camped for the winter about a mile from the town at a place called Falmouth. The Confederates remained in position at Fredericksburg, so the two armies with the Rappahannock River between them, were just waiting for spring to come. Eli said the river was the "Dare Mark" which they dared one another to cross. He expressed the desire to leave the area however, since they had burned all the wood they could find in the area. They were finally reduced to burning old field pine bushes or oak wood that had to be dragged over half a mile. He said that that part of the county was ruined since all the timber there had been cut down.

According to Eli's letter of March 17th, the fighting had begun and the big battle would soon begin:

> *Dear Mother,*
> *I once more seat myself to write you a few lines which will inform you that I am in good health. I wrote you the other day but I thought I would write again as I thought perhaps I might not have the chance soon again for we are now expecting active service now every day. I think when you hear from us again you will hear of a bloody time. The winter is nearly over and the summer is near. The fighting must begin soon or it is not to begin at all. It has begun for they are fighting now in hearing of us. There has been a continual cannonading all day*

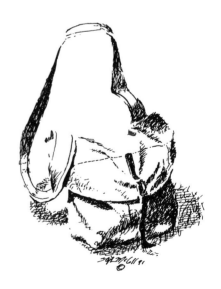

*up the river from here but it's several miles off but I am listening every minute for them to call on us for reinforcements. I think from the way the cannons roar it must be a very hard struggle. But don't let this cause you any uneasiness for such things can't be hoped for the fighting must be done. This war was forced on us by the proud fanatics of the nation. Now we can only resist it with the ball and bayonet and let us do it courageously if we die in the attempt. Let us implore the mercy of God to be with us in such trying times.*

In an earlier letter written in February, Eli told of the Yankees having a new commander. He said, " I would not be surprised if we don't have some very hard fighting before long for the Yankeys has got a new commander and he will want to do something extra." This new commander was General Joe Hooker, who replaced Burnside. He spent the winter reorganizing his troops and restocking equipment and supplies. He had in his camp over one hundred and twenty five thousand men while Lee had only sixty thousand.

Hooker's plan of attack was put into action on April 27th with one group moving east of Fredericksburg to draw attention away from the actual place he planned to attack. He then secretly moved his main army to Chancellorsville, a small town nearby. It seemed Hooker's plan was going to be successful in defeating Lee since he had the Confederates surrounded and was forcing them to fight on his terms. General Lee, however, learned of Hooker's plan and turned to face him. By marching quickly all night, he encountered Hooker's troops before they could get to their chosen place of battle, which would have given them the advantage. Hooker backed off and Lee took their position, but put himself and his men in a dangerous position with Union troops in front as well as in back of his lines.

Lee's strategy was to outmaneuver the Union forces. He did this by making them think that Stonewall Jackson was retreating. Jackson's men did retreat for a distance, but then turned to come in at the right flank of the Federals, surprising them with heavy cannon and musket fire. The Union troops were taken totally by surprise and could not stand up against Jackson's troops. Hooker, who was so confident that his plan was working, couldn't believe it when he saw his men retreating from the line.

Nightfall brought a temporary halt to the fighting, but Jackson decided to go out with some of his staff on a reconnaissance of Federal lines for a night attack. He left his men lining both sides of the plank road with orders to shoot anyone coming down the road. When he came upon a line of Union infantry lying in wait, he turned and rode back down the road, unmindful of his previous order to shoot. As he approached in the dim, fog-shrouded night, his own men opened fire on him and he fell from his horse severely wounded. He died a few days later. In a brief note written by Eli on the margin of a letter to his sister he said, "Our great General Jackson is dead. Our own men shot him through a mistake on Saturday night. I just hope we can find another Jackson."

Jackson's death was mourned not only by Southern troops, but by Federal troops as well, who respected him for the great general that he was.

General Sedgwick began marching toward the Confederate troops stationed up on Marye's Heights. At the foot of this high ground stood the same stone wall that had been a death trap for so many at the battle of Fredricksburg. After several attempts to scale the hill, Sedgewick's troops finally succeeded taking their objective, but many men were lost in the attempt. By nightfall, the Union controlled both cross-over places on the Rappahannock and Rapidan Rivers. This would give them access to a safe crossing if necessary. Lee gathered his troops' last remaining strength and forced Sedgwick and Hooker to retreat across to the northern side of the river. The trenches were full of the bodies of men in both blue and gray. The Union counted seventeen thousand killed and wounded, the Confederates thirteen thousand. It was all over on May 5th, with the Union troops back at Falmouth and the Confederates in camp at Fredericksburg. Eli's letter of May 8th describes the carnage he had witnessed:

101

*My Dear Mother,*

*Knowing that you will be uneasy till you hear from me I will write to you for you will be sure to hear that I was killed in the fight last Sunday, for it was currently reported here that I was. But I write this with my own hand to testify that I am yet in the Land of the Living and all honor and glory be to God for his care over me. We have had some awful times here for the last ten days. We have been in line of battle all the time marching through the woods, mud, and swamps and some part of the army was fighting all the time. We have lost a many a good soldier during this time. The 3rd of May our Brigade got into it heels over head and our regiment lost more men than we ever have in arry fight yet. We had to fight them behind their entrenchments. There was some of our company killed within fifteen steps of their trench. Our company is nearly ruined. At last count we had lost three killed dead on the field, and twenty wounded I will give you the names of some of the wounded: Asa Wright, Frank Plaster, Thom Mathews, Dave Johnson, Dave Rutledge, Jo Rutledge, Thom Todd, Thom Massey, Jim Raby, Bill Hunneycutt, Caut Cofer and others. Bill Wommack lost his right leg and died soon after. Thom Massey lost his left arm. Thom Weathers was wounded and died the next day. Elbert Daniels got shot through the thigh and also died soon after. I was slightly wounded in the hand but I am still with the company. I stayed at the hospital two days to wait on Jim Mathews and Bill Wommack. They was badly wounded. Jim was shot near the kidneys. The ball never come out and he was very feeble when I left him. I understand he died today, poor fellow said all the time it would kill him. He said that a plain token come to him that if he went into the fight he would get killed. The poor fellow looked very pitiful at me when he got shot and begged me to help him but I had no time to lose. It was everyman for himself for they was falling on my right and left and my disposition inclined to try to return the fire with as much injury as possible. We fought desperately to gain the day but after all our destruction we captured the whole passel of the line that was fighting us. They raised from their trench with a white flag and surrendered to us like lambs. Three cheers for the Army of the Potomac! I must brag although our Brigade suffered worse than any other but my heart is full of thanks for the great skill that has been manifested among us. During the fight we have defeated the enemy.In every attempt we have completed our designated goal and every point we have slain thousands of their men.There is no use to try to give a correct report of the prisoners though I don't think that fifteen thousand will cover the number we have taken. Several of their generals and many officers of other ranks as well. Our troops all seemed to go into it as cheerful as if they was going to their dinner and not very few stragglers behind either. The men would march with their heads up and energy shining on their brows and with such a spirit the victory will always be ours. We have drove old Hooker and his blue coats back over the Dare Mark, but thousands of them will never get back. They will moulder on the south side of the River. The Rappahannock River is the Dare Mark with General Lee they can't stay on this side!*

Eli lost another one of his friends in this battle and wrote to his mother about it afterward.

*Just before the fight E.N. Payne of our Co got him a nice coverlid and said that he was going to keep it till he could see his brother, a wagoner, and he could take care of it for him till winter. He said he would need it then but the poor fellow needed it in a few hours for his shroud.I tell you Dear Mother a man has no promise of his life therefore we aught to be preparing to be ready to meet the call at any and all times for everything bears witness to the fact that there is a certain time and doom affixed for one and all. We all need the Countersign to enter the Eternal Campaign above. As I aforesaid, I aught to be thankful for my past fortune for since the war began there has been seven of my mess died killed and wounded while I here yet almost untouched. It seems like losing one of a family to lose one out of the mess.*

103

Desertion from the army was a problem right from the beginning of the war but grew progressively worse as the war dragged on. In a letter written in April, 1862, it seems to have been occurring in Eli's camp at Yorktown. He said:

> *A man is in danger of his life to leave the camp and the orders that was given to pickets that relieved us this morning was that if any man run or give orders to run without orders from the commanding officers, he is to be shot.*

In another instance he said that "Four or five of this brigade deserted and when they brought them back they looked like they was sent for and could not come. They are now under guard waiting for their trial."

In another letter he described the procedure for executing the deserters:

> *There is one of the 10th Georgia Regiment to be shot to death with musketry tomorrow for deserting his colors in time of battle. It is bad enough to be shot without the name of deserting. Bud Nash has deserted. He has been gone about one month. He run out of fights just as long as he could without being courtmartialed so I reckon he thought he would leave for good. But he might a been gone long ago for all the good he has ever done. I do reckon I've as little sympathy for a deserter as anybody in the world!*

McLaw's Division, of which Eli's regiment was a part, was not in the central part of the battle, but held a position at a point known today as McLaw's Road. Here they held back Union reinforcements from coming in from the south. Even though they were not in the thick of battle, they saw enough action to have lost a number of men. Eli wrote to his mother on May 17th to tell her about it:

> *Dear Mother,*
> *This beautiful Sabbath morning I take great pleasure in*

*answering your very kind letter I read yesterday evening. I was glad to hear from you all. I was glad to hear that you was getting along with your work in your little farm. I hope you may be able to cultivate and procure a handsome living at home. I feel confident that you will. I am not digesting well this morning. My bowels has been deranged for sometime with dysentery though I am not a past doing duty. Excuse this bad writing for the pen and paper is both sorry. I am sorry that you have been so uneasy about me for I wrote you the first opportunity after the battle knowing that you would be uneasy tell you heard from me. I also wrote to some of my friends requesting them to tell you the news. but I hope you have heard from me by this time. The good news is that I come through safe. I am under Ten Thousand renewed obligations to be thankful for my past fortune. What remains for the future none of us is able to tell. It is useless for me to go on and tell all about the fight for if you read my last letter you can get a small idea of the affairs. It is over with now. The enemy was badly whiped and panic stricken. But it was done with great slaughter on both sides. We lost many of our boys. I tell you the old 16th looks quite small since the fight. Our company looks like a platoon. We only have thirty six men present in the company. We have plenty of tents and room now so many killed and wounded and left their places vacant. Everytime we form the company it makes me feel bad to see so many vacant places in ranks. To think where we left some of them lying dead in the woods. The Dreadful Sword of Death has trimmed them from our ranks*

*"Mamma, I bought a nice double-cased watch for 30 dollars. I thought I had as well have a good watch as have the money, for if I should ever have the bad luck to be a prisoner, it would be worth more than money and I always had to borrow one when I was on guard."*
*March, 1863*

Eli had attained the rank of Sergeant by the time he fought at Chancellorsville and was listed among the casualties as having an injured hand. In the letter that he wrote to his mother following the battle, however, he didn't mention the injury, knowing that she would worry about him. Instead, he blamed the poor quality of his penmanship on a "sorry" pen and poor quality paper.

Events were now building toward the next big clash of the two armies at the little town of Gettysburg.

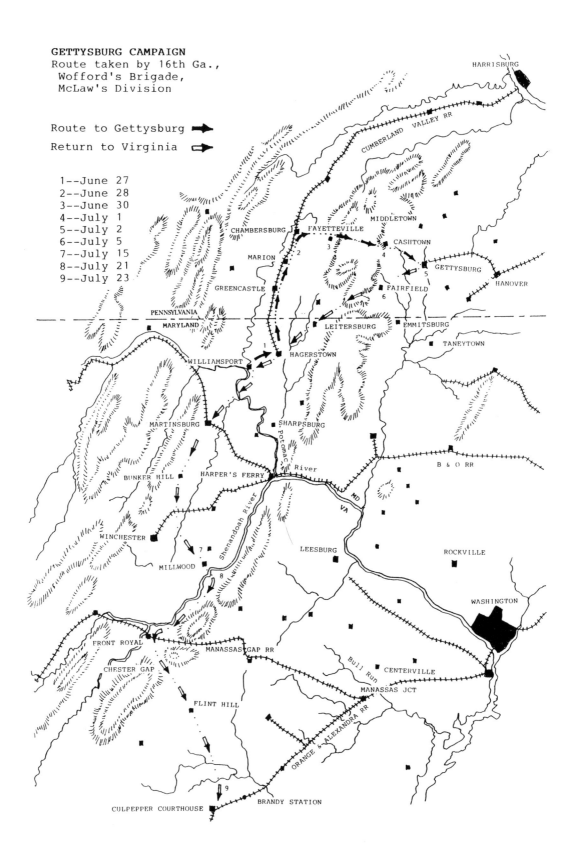

**GETTYSBURG CAMPAIGN**
Route taken by 16th Ga.,
Wofford's Brigade,
McLaw's Division

Route to Gettysburg ➡
Return to Virginia ⇨

1--June 27
2--June 28
3--June 30
4--July 1
5--July 2
6--July 5
7--July 15
8--July 21
9--July 23

HARRISBURG

CUMBERLAND VALLEY RR

MIDDLETOWN

CHAMBERSBURG    FAYETTEVILLE    CASHTOWN
                2          3        4
MARION                                   GETTYSBURG
                                    5
GREENCASTLE                              HANOVER
                          FAIRFIELD
                          6
PENNSYLVANIA
MARYLAND        LEITERSBURG    EMMITSBURG
                                    TANEYTOWN
                1
        WILLIAMSPORT    HAGERSTOWN

                        SHARPSBURG

                        Potomac

MARTINSBURG                            B & O RR

                        River

BUNKER HILL    HARPER'S FERRY
                                MD
                                VA

WINCHESTER                              ROCKVILLE
                        LEESBURG
        7  Shenandoah River

MILLWOOD

        8                              WASHINGTON

FRONT ROYAL    MANASSAS GAP RR
                                CENTERVILLE
CHESTER GAP
                                MANASSAS JCT
        FLINT HILL              Bull Run

                    ORANGE & ALEXANDRA RR

        9
CULPEPPER COURTHOUSE    BRANDY STATION

## Chapter VII

## The Beginning of the End at Gettysburg

LEE'S NEXT MAJOR OBJECTIVE was to hit the Union in its own territory, taking the conflict out of the South for a while. His sights were set on Harrisburg, Pennsylvania, the railroad center bringing supplies to the Federals. In early June, Eli's regiment was stationed near Culpepper Courthouse in northern Virginia and seemed to be moving slowly northward, but with no particular destination in mind. His letter of June 11th contained mostly news about his health and concern for his family, but he did indicate that though there had been a few minor skirmishes, there were none of real importance. He felt however, that their leisurely pace was permitting them a chance to rest for what was soon to come.

In his letter of June 11th from Culpepper Courthouse he speculates on where he will be going:

> *I want you to write soon and give me all the news one more time before we take another trip into Maryland which we all think is very eminent. We believe that is where we have started and I dread the trip, but I went there once and it is not impossible to do it again. I don't know when I will have the chance to write again, and don't be uneasy about me.*

On a small scrap of paper he scribbled notes mapping their route into northern territory:

*Here is the names of the towns we have been in since we come back in the U.S. This is the greatest wheat country in the world. I never saw the likes.*

*June 26th into Maryland. Went through Williamsport. Crossed the Potomac River*

Today, this is roughly the route taken by Interstate 81.

*27th through Hagerstown, Maryland*
*Middleway PA*

*Greencastle PA*

*28th Marion PA*

*Chambersburg PA*

*30th through Faitville PA - turned east toward Gettysburg*

*July lst in the night through Cashtown. Turned south, circling around Gettysburg*

*July 5th through Fairfax PA*

*26th through Waterloo PA*

*26th through Lightensburg MD*

*26th back through Hagerstown MD*

*"This is a splendid country. Everything is in plenty. The people here has never felt the War in their country till now."*
June, 1863

The next letter was written on June 28th from Chambersburg, Pennsylvania:

*We crossed into Maryland on the 26th but we only stayed one night in that state. We only come through one corner of it. We have been marching on Pennsylvania soil for two days and our division is in the rear of the army. Some of the troops is a long ways from here. Ahead of us they are near the capital of this state. We aim to take it before long. We have had a long hard march since I wrote you last and some very hot weather. It was very severe on us soldiers but for the last ten days it has been*

108

more pleasant. The soldiers is getting more used to it. There's hardly any sickness or straggling in the army for the last few days but during them hot days there was hundreds of our boys fainted and fell in the road and many of them died but I have been able to keep up all the way. We have a large army now in Pennsylvania and it is in good fix and fine spirits. We intend to let the Yankey Nation feel the sting of the War as our borders has ever since the war begun. The citizens takes it very well. They are almost scared to death but we treat them very well. Our officer has pressed in a vast quantity of Government Property of all kinds, some of the finest horses I ever saw and some of the finest beeves you ever saw. We draw plenty of good beef now. We intend to press all we can while we are in the Union. Us soldiers treats the people with respects when we want anything and we offer them our money for it and if they refuse it we just take it at our own price. I sent my watch home by Mr. Shamblee and I am sorry I done so. If I had it now I could turn it in for $100. of our money for I could sell it for Yankey money and then I could get things as cheap here as we ever could in Georgia. This is a splendid country. Everything is plenty. The people has never felt the war in their country till now. The Yankeys is mighty troubled about this movement of our army. They are calling out the militia in a hurry to defend the capital but if they don't mind we will get there before their militia does. We have only marched six miles today. We have stopped to rest and cook up rations and get the Government Property out at town. We will have some hard fighting before long. We need not expect anything else but I hope we will be successful. Don't be uneasy about me. I will do the best I can for myself. If you don't hear from me in a month don't be uneasy for there will be no chance to send a letter but I will let you hear from me as often as I can while we stay in the U.S.

*"I have seen a heap of pretty Yankee girls but somehow I can't help but hate them. Tell them that I say that Yankey girls looks mighty well but I love them [at home] the best."*
Pennsylvania, 1863

It appears from the letter that the troops still had Harrisburg as their goal, not suspecting that the battle would take place at a town called Gettysburg. Eli's sense of the Confederacy already being a separate nation is evident as he refers to land above the Mason-Dixon Line as the United States.

The main vanguard of Lee's army never got to Harris-

burg because a small squad of men had left the main group to go into the quiet Pennsylvania town of Gettysburg in search of shoes for their barefoot men. They ran into a Yankee patrol there and shots were exchanged. Both sides sent in reinforcements and the result was a three day battle from July lst to the 3rd. It ended as one of the most costly battles of the war with over fifty thousand men killed and wounded. Lee's troops limped back across the border into Virginia. This battle was the turning point for the Confederacy. From this point on it was clear that the South was losing the war.

There is a large gap in the sequence of Eli's letters at this point. They could have been lost through the years, or it might have been that Eli couldn't take the time to write as often as he had in the past. Even though he doesn't write about the great battle at Gettysburg, we know he was there because in one of his letters he mentions picking up a little silver spoon for a souvenir:

*Tell little Charles that I sent him a little Yankey spoon by Sam Dyer. I got it off of the Bloody Battlefield of Pennsylvania. Tell him he must not lose it. He must keep it to remember his old Unkle E.P. I wish I had some little thing to send all the children but I've nothing but love.*

There are no letters from Eli describing the route the Sixteenth Regiment took back into Virginia. However, J.H. Reinhardt, another member of the Sixteenth Regiment, tells where they went after the battle:

*We crossed a pontoon bridge 7 miles from Martinsburg where we rested and got food. We only got l meal a day.*

*July l5th—Marched through Martinsburg, through Dartsville to Burke Hill, twelve miles from Winchester where we stayed until the 20th. Then headed toward Millwood near Paris Gap.*

*July 2lst - Headed to Front Royal and crossed the Shenandoah River on pontoon bridges. We camped there for the night.*

*July 22nd -Headed to Gains Cross Roads and crossed the mountains at Chester Gap. We saw some Yankees on a hill to the left. They began firing at our wagons. Wofford's Brigade [Eli's unit] was ordered to attack them at l0:PM. They ran the Yankees off and we camped for the night. [Note: This was probably the skirmish near Snicker's Gap.]*

*July 23rd - We left today for Culpepper Courthouse where we camped near the railroad getting much needed rest.*

The next extant letter from Eli that there is any record of was dated July 3lst from Culpepper Courthouse, Virginia. There is no mention of any fighting and contains references to relatives and conditions at home. He mentions again how good it would be to go back home again and says:

*"I've got a very bad cold after washing yesterday. I washed my clothes and had to go without a shirt till it got dry. I wore the skin off my hands rubbing. I washed 2 shirts, 1 pair of drawers, and 1 pair of pants. I hung them out to dry and some fellow took one of my shirts off of the bush so I lost the shirt and my labor and had to buy another one.*
August, 1863

*Oh how glad I would be to roll up to my old sweet home one more time. If I had it, I would give $500. to be at home for two months, but it is very uncertain whether I will ever see it again or not but I hope my resolution will hold out to stay till I can come up boldly and not have to be concealed. My mind is so confused.....*

At another place in this letter he does mention that the artillery had begun to move again and that they were uneasy about the Federal troops coming down toward Atlanta, so they didn't expect to be staying there much longer. Their purpose for being in this area was to protect the Orange and Alexandria Railroad which connected Richmond with the rich Shenandoah Valley, the source of much-needed supplies for Confederate troops in the east.

In his letter of August 10th, Eli mentions some confrontations with the enemy but doesn't specify where they occur. He tells about some of his friends being taken prisoner and says that they were being treated badly. He talks about the "Black Flag" being flown, which meant that there would be "no quarter given" when capturing an enemy. No one would be taken alive:

*They have got many of our friends in their hands and they are beginning to treat them very bad. I would not be surprised no time to hear of the Black Flag being raised on that account. There is some talk of it but I hope the people will use more humanity in this war than that. I am willing to defend our rights under a Civilized Banner, but I am very much opposed to the Black Flag. But if the Yankees raises it first I will fight it but if our men raises it first then I am done. Give all the Vicksburg boys my best respects. Tell them to keep in heart but I know it is bad to fight under officers without confidence. I wish they had such officers as we have got. I think they would be more successful. General Lee has the confidence of our whole army. We don't doubt his loyalty.*

Eli's next two letters were written in Spotsylvania County, Virginia. In them he reports that there is little activity on the battlefield and he grows more philosophical in its

*"It makes me feel very bad just to think how many of my old associates is gone and they are all experiencing Eternity while I am yet on the Terms of Time and Probation."*
August 28, 1863

*"All military duty is suspended for today. President Davis has proclaimed this day for fasting and prayer throughout the whole Confederacy, but I think the most of the boys eats a heap and prays but little, but I believe that we will have to be more obedient than we are before we can expect to be delivered from this state of trouble. We will have to deny our strength and acknowledge the Almighty's."*
August, 1863

remarks:

> *Dear Mother,*
> *I received your letter of the 17th the other evening which found me well and this also leaves me well. Everything is silent at this time. No prospect for an immediate engagement about here. We are enjoying a good long rest which we all very much need. I was sorry to hear of the death of our Preacher Teat. I was in hopes to hear him preach again but I'm in hopes and verily believe that he is gone home to receive the great reward that is promised the faithful, which ought to encourage us all to try to become one of that party knowing the time is swiftly rolling on when we will receive that great pension or the Fate of Condemnation. We have Divine Services in the regiment every night and I am glad to see the soldiers take such great interest in it as they do. We all should appreciate and improve the time and opportunities for no time is promised to us, only the present. What a great blessing we will have at preaching tonight in our street. We have a Presbyterian for our Chaplain.*

> *Dear Mother,*
> *It appears that you are very uneasy about me and I would rather you would reconcile yourself about me forever. A friend that is able and will stand by me in every hour and article of Tribulation though you may never see me again. I wish I was there with you but I can wish only. I hope to see the Eagle of Peace stretch forth her wings one day. You must excuse this short letter and accept it as a token of love and respect. Write when you can. I can't hear from you all too often.*

*"Everything is silent at this time. No prospect for an immediate engagement here. We are enjoying a good long rest which we all very much needed."*
Spotsylvania Cty. Va.
August, 1863

In a letter written to his sister Caroline on the same day, he told about foraging for food in the northern Virginia countryside:

> *You spoke about you and Cousin Lou and Sallie making cider. I woulda liked very much to hope you for fruit is very scarce indeed about here but we drew some apples yesterday. A man just made a sacrifice of his orchard and give up the fruit to our Brigade and they made a detail to gather them and divide*

*them. There was about 1 dozen to the man and it was a large orchard so you can give a guess what few chances we all have by the time all gets some. But I was in a rich streak the other day but we had to move camps and that broke me up. I was on guard at a house two or three days where they had plenty of peaches and apples and three of the nicest kind of young ladies you had better believe! I enjoyed myself well. The people was as kind as they could be and upon the whole of it, I fell in love with one of the old gent's daughters. I think her superior to anything I've found in Virginia. I tell you the sun comes down very hot on us but we have built a large arbor to shade under. We get plenty to eat since we've got in regular camps. Our diet is corn bread and beef and sometimes bacon. The boys don't like the cornbread much. It is too hard to cook. Our army is badly scattered from Fredericksburg to Orange Courthouse. We are about halfway between but there is not much chance to forage about through the country after vegetables or refreshments of any kind. The Provo guards will arrest every man they find from camps without a pass from the General. General McLaws has ordered a market house near our camps and for all citizens to bring all the poultry they can spare to that place, there to be paid a reasonable price for it. Soldiers is not allowed to get anything only from that place but I don't think that will be much advantage. Remember I am your brother as ever.*

The last letter written from Virginia came from Spotsylvania County on September 5th. Apparently the letters from home had been few and far between and Eli seemed to feel that he had been forgotten: "I've not heard from you since the 17th of August. I'm anxious to hear from you all again. My old Gwinnett friends has forgotten me. They have quit writing!"

In just a few days, the Sixteenth Regiment would receive orders to move south to Georgia to help the beleaguered troops of Braxton Bragg defend their state. It would be there that Eli's final chapter would be written.

## Chapter VIII
## *The End of the Road at Chickamauga*

AFTER THE BATTLE of Gettysburg, the two armies sat scowling at each other as if they were just too tired to fight anymore. The remainder of 1863 was relatively quiet in the East, but the western theater began to heat up again. Chattanooga, Tennessee became the focal point for the Federals, since control of it would afford them passage into Georgia and the Deep South. It was also a major rail center that linked Tennessee with other parts of the Confederacy. General Rosecrans and a force of sixty thousand Federals pursued Braxton Bragg and his troops back into Georgia to a place called Chickamauga. On the 19th, Longstreet and a large number of Confederate troops, including the sixteenth Georgia, arrived from Virginia to assist them. Together, they smashed through the Union line pushing Rosecrans back toward Chattanooga. Eli wrote to his mother about the battle on September 24th from a camp near Chattanooga, Tennessee:

*"We had a jolly time coming down from Virginia but I hated to leave the old state after doing so much hard service in it and it seems like we are away from home. I shall always respect old Virginia and her people."*
September, 1863

> *Dear Mother,*
> *Knowing that you are very anxious to hear from me I will write you a few lines which will inform you that I am well this morning. There has been some very hard fighting since our Virginia army has arrived here but our Brigade has not been in no fight yet, more than skirmishing. Our troops has been very successful so far. We have drove the enemy some eight or ten miles and cleared them off of Georgia soil, killing a great many of them and taking many prisoners but the number has not been ascertained yet but I saw twenty two hundred in one*

115

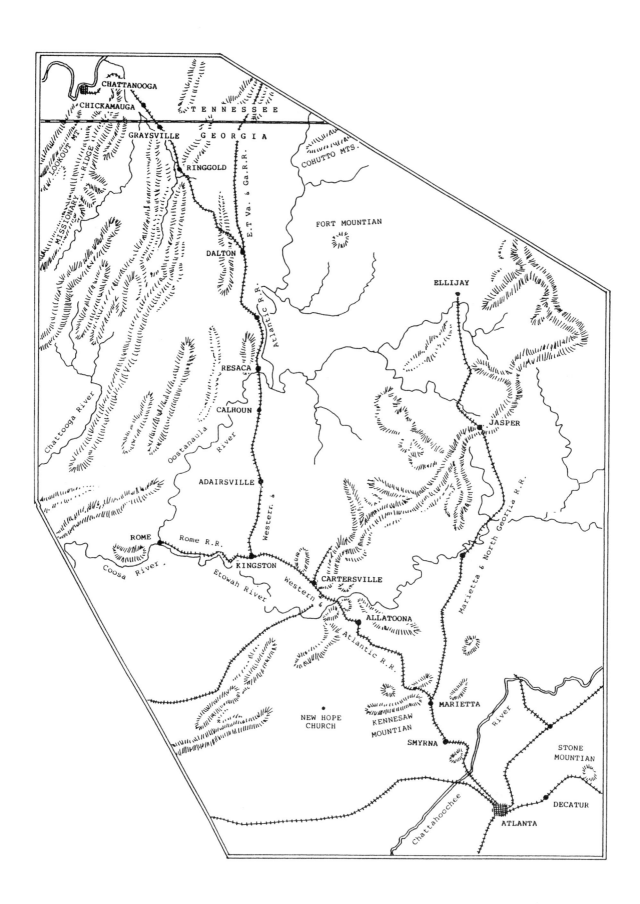

*drove. Our Virginia troops fights like tigers up here in the West. They say they are going to show them the lick it is done with but I think the Western boys is all right. They are not as bad whipt as we heard they was. They all seem to be in good spirits. The Yankeys has fell back to Chattanooga to their entrenchments. They are well fortified and we are in the line of battle, both parties near each other. It is thought that if we can't flank their position some way that we will have to charge them out of their works and if we do it will be done with great slaughter on our side. There is no other chance for they have got good cannon and rifle works but I hope there will be some way for our Prosperity. I will say no more about the fight till it is over with if I should live to see the end. I like this part of the country very well but the weather is dry dry. The dust in the roads is shoe mouth deep and when marching the dust rises so thick a person can hardly see his way. We had a jolly time coming from Virginia but I hated to leave the old state after doing so much hard service in it and it seems like we are away from home. I shall always respect old Virginia and her people. Excuse this short letter for we are in line of battle now and not much time for writing. Don't be uneasy about me.*

The movement of fifteen thousand troops from Virginia was difficult since they traveled in old, overloaded train cars. They were packed, not only in passenger cars, but also in boxcars, flatcars, and baggage cars. It was so hot they had to tear off the sidings in order to keep from suffocating. Many of the tracks had different gauges, which ran very short distances and necessitated unloading from one line and then re-loading to another one, so it took a total of seven days and sixteen railroad lines to get them from Richmond, Virginia to northern Georgia! One of the change- over places was Atlanta, which Eli mentioned in his letter of September 24th:

*I was sadly disappointed not seeing some of you when we got to Atlanta. Most all the boys when they got off the train was meeting their relations and I kept looking among thousands for some of mine but narry one could I find. But I saw a good many of my old friends which was a great satisfaction to me. I saw Thom Hutchins and S. McDaniel, Haymie Liddell and several others. Dear Mother I tell you it was a trying case for me to pass so near home and not call but I pondered the matter. I thought sufficiently and thought it was my duty to stick to the company, deny myself, forsake home for the present and cleave to the cause of our bleeding country to drive the oppressors from our soil which threatens our own door. I thought we was badly needed or we would not a been sent for. I knew it would not be much pleasure for me to beat home without leave. I may never see you nor my home again but if I never do I can't help it. I expect to be a man of Honor to our country at the risk of my life. I don't want to be a disgrace to myself nor my relations.*

Eli's mother and sister Caroline did in fact try to see him at the station in Atlanta, but missed him because of delays they met on the road from Yellow River. He found out about this when a letter arrived from Caroline a few days later:

*E.P. we are about twenty miles from you this morning. We will come as close to the lines as we dare and we wish you to come out and see us if you can this evening. If you can't we will stay there or you hide until you can come. We will come on the canal once today. We did not know you were fighting when we started from home, Be sure and come out this evening or night. We are all well. All the boys is coming next week. I never wanted to see any person so bad in my life. I can't go back home without seeing you. We went to Atlanta to get you but you was done gone. I never did hate anything so bad. We left home Monday morning but we have been delayed on the way on account of so many soldiers. We are at the station this side of Ringgold and we will start towards you on the ambulance in the morning. The train can get no further. If I thought we would not get to see you I would write more. I hope we will find some time to get to see you.*

The last letter from Eli was written on October 2nd, the contents

of which indicate that his sister and mother did get to visit him. Something had happened to him in that short interval since they had seen him however, and he was apparently very sick. His letter was very difficult to decipher since the writing was almost illegible, quite unlike any others he had previously written:

> *Rossville,Georgia*
> *Oct 2nd 1863*
>
> *Dear Mother,*
> *I reckon you will hear that I am very sick and I have been but I am getting better. I got worse all the time after you left. Day before yesterday was a very wet day and I come very near going out. The ground was covered in water everything wet no place to lie down. I got so bad that they started me to the hospital through the rain and I got as far as Mr. Lemmons. I just felt like I was going to die so I went in and just told them I must stay there. They soon fixed my bed and done all they could for me. Next morning come maybe we can come on here. In a few days I am going back to the company for I get no better fare here than I do there. Don't be uneasy about me and come back. I was afraid that some of the boys would write that I was very sick but I am a heap better. Most well so don't be uneasy.*
> *E.P. Landers*

Looking back to his letter of September 24th, one wonders if somehow he had a premonition of his death, because unlike any other letter he had written up until this time, he talked of death and what arrangements he wanted for his burial:

> *It is unknown who will get killed in this fight. It may be me and if I do get killed if there is any chance I want my body taken up and laid in the dust round old Sweetwater and I want a tombstone put at my head with my name and my company and regiment, the day I enlisted and the name and date of all the*

*battles I have ever been in. I have spoke to some of the company to see to this matter if they should live and me not. I reckon what little I've got will pay expenses. This is my request if it is possible. Now don't think I've give up to being killed but you know it is an uncertain thing as we are expecting to be called to attention soon so I will hasten through.*

According to Clement Eaton, the renowned Civil War historian, Eli's request for a tombstone of this type was typical of that era because young men of that period believed that it would insure his living forever in the memory of his relatives, remembered as having been one who died bravely for a patriotic cause. It was believed that if a boy died for his country, the glory was his forever.

Eli's fondest wish was to return to Gwinnett County to his family and friends. He wanted to be able to roam the fields on his mare, Jane, and plow the fields with his mule Kate. He wanted to marry a Gwinnett girl and lead the simple life he had known before the war. This wasn't to be however, and though he did return, it was not in the way he had hoped. He died October 27, 1863. The military record simply states that Eli died of disease. However, in a small notation in the family bible, his mother wrote the following note: "E.P. Landers died October 27, 1863. A true soldier always stood up to his post. Died in Rome Ga. with the tiford[sic, probably typhoid] fever. Aged 21 years. In a letter written by Daniel Minor, Eli's brother-in-law, dated October 20th—a few days before Eli's death—Minor writes that Eli is very sick:

*Chickamauga, Tennessee*
*October 20, 1863*

*Dear Son,*
*I take my pen this morning to let you all know that I am not right well. I have got a bad cold. I have stood in the rain three days and nights, ankle deep. I am better this morning. I hope these lines will find you all well. We are now on the road to*

*Charleston, Tenn., they say, but I don't know where they will go to. They had a fight about Chattanooga. We whipped them bad. I can hear the cannons roaring every day It is cold at night and I stand cold when on guard and lie cold sometimes in a mud hole. It is bad. It is clear now. I have dried all my things. I think I can sleep tonight, if we don't travel. Daniel, Eli Landers says he wants to see you all. He could tell you a heap. Poor fellow! He sees hard times. This water does not agree with him, nor Bob neither. When I get a letter from home, you can let me know how they are a faring and where they are. I must close. So I remain*
*Father 'till death,*
*Daniel Minor*

This was to be the last letter Dan Minor wrote. He died from pneumonia in Tennessee soon afterwards.

Eli's sickness progressed very rapidly. On September 24th he was well. By October 2nd he was critically ill. He would die two weeks later. In November, Longstreet's troops met the strong Federal forces at Knoxville, so maybe Eli's untimely death spared him much suffering.

His body was returned home and laid to rest in the churchyard beside his beloved Sweetwater Church. He rests there today on the Lawrenceville Highway with cars streaming past in a never-ending procession, their occupants hardly casting an eye at the lone grave there on the hill. Now that his story has been told, perhaps the people of his native Gwinnett County, as well as all those who read his story, will appreciate what this simple farm boy sacrificed for his people and his convictions.

The Confederate soldier was truly dedicated to the cause for which he fought. He very willingly he answered the call to duty. In the words of the historian Carlton McCarthy, "The romance of war charmed him and he hurried from the embrace of his mother to the embrace of death."

# *EPILOGUE*

BOOKS ARE FILLED with stories of heroes who have done great and glorious things to deserve that title, yet one seldom remembers the names of those who were common soldiers. Such a one was Eli P.Landers, the subject of this work, who fought so desperately day in and day out under the most adverse conditions. Does one have to do something really spectacular to earn the title of hero? Was Eli Landers a hero? Is his story worthy of a place in history? We believe that it is.

Eli Landers left a sheltered, protected environment to go and courageously fight for a cause he believed in. His forthright, honest nature shone forth in his feelings about soldiers deserting the army after pledging loyalty, a route he would never take, though it must have been tempting at times. His concern about repaying his debts even though the army seldom paid him enough to buy the bare essentials of life was a reflection of his deep honesty and natural integrity. Sitting up with dying comrades when he could have been getting rest for his own body revealed the loyalty and love that was so typical of him.

These letters that lay fogotten for over a century in a dusty attic, have opened a fresh perspective on the war as seen through the eyes of one who lived it. There are few spectacular revelations in them and few famous names. They are simply the observations and descriptions of a nineteen-year-old country boy from the North Georgia hill country who was away from home for the first time in his life. Accustomed to a loving, gentle family, he was thrown into an alien environment that eventually destroyed him. Eli's real enemy, as was that of so many others in the Confederate army, was not the opposing army, but disease, inclement weather, and improper and inadequate food. Through all the hardships he endured however, there was always an abiding faith in God, and the deep conviction that God would always be there to sustain him.

Yes, Eli Landers was a hero. Though he lies in a forgotten graveyard, he lives on in these letters with words that can inspire us all to stand up for what we truly believe in. If heroes survive through time, it's because they, like Eli Landers, stand firmly on the rock of their convictions and values.

## *Appendix I*
## *The Landers Family*

IN THE YEAR 1729, Luke Landers and his wife, Rachel Paris, moved from Hanover County, Virginia to Granville County, North Carolina. Two of their sons, John and Tyree, served in the American Revolution. After the war was over, Tyree married Frances Davis and in 1790, they moved from North Carolina to Elbert County, Georgia. He founded several Primitive Baptist churches in that area, as well as the Sweetwater Church in Gwinnett County, which later had such a great influence on the life of Eli Landers. Tyree's proficiency in writing was a source of pride to him and his family and his talents were handed down to his children and grandchildren. This was evident in the writing of his grandson, Eli. It helps account for the ease with which Eli wrote and expressed himself, since there was a scarcity of schools in the early 19th century, and a large majority of the population, particularly in remote rural areas, were uneducated. Eli prized his ability to write and mentioned how glad he was to have the "gift of the pen."

Tyree's son, Humphrey Davis Landers was born in 1788. He grew up in Elbert County, Georgia, but after he married Sarah Browner, he moved to Gwinnett County, about eight miles west of the town of Lawrenceville. The family were staunch Baptists, and Humphrey gave two acres of his land on which to build the Sweetwater Primitive Baptist Church and for its cemetery.

Humphrey's wife, Sarah, gave birth to eight children, but in 1831, soon after the birth of her last child, she died, leaving him with five small children, whose ages ranged from one year to eleven years of age. That same year, Humphrey

Davis Landers married Susan McDaniel, a woman much younger than himself and by her, fathered eight more children. He died in 1846, leaving Susan with the responsibility of raising this large family by herself. Two of her children had died in infancy, but the six remaining children ranged in ages from two years to thirteen years. She also had one of Humphrey's children by his first wife, Humphrey Davis, still living at home as well. In 1851, however, he married a local girl, Wealthy Fowler, and moved with some of his older brothers and sisters to Randolph County, Alabama.

The remaining children of Susan's were Harriet, Napoleon, Elizabeth, Rebecca Adaline, Eli Pinson, and Huldy Caroline. All of them were married at the outbreak of the Civil War except Eli and Carolina.

This family was close-knit, and on the morning that Eli left for Virginia after he had enlisted in the army, his brother, Napoleon ("Pole"), and his brother-in-law, "Moten" Hutchins, went to see him off at the station. Eli remarked later how they stayed by him until the train began to move and said how sad he was to leave them.

Napoleon was twenty-seven years old when Eli enlisted. He was apparently in poor health at that time and did not go with the first group of volunteers from Gwinnett County. After Eli got settled into camp in Richmond, he must have heard that his brother was planning to join up in spite of his condition, because he tried to discourage him from doing so. He wrote a letter to him and said,

> *Pole, don't you volunteer for God's sake for I know enough about camps to know that your constitution ain't strong enough to stand camp life. This is no place for a weakly man to be for they can't be favored in their weakness. If they ain't right sick they have to go the same as a stout man and don't you volunteer. That is my request as a brother that wishes you will take care of Mamma for I can't be there to do it. Pole, take my advice for it is good.*

He later restated these feelings in a letter to his mother:

*I know Pole's condition and I know our conditions and I know he couldn't undergo the hardships that is put upon us here and if he could only hear the dying groans that I have heard on account of being exposed to the cold so much, he would stay at home. If he will only take my advice he will not regret it in a day. Notwithstanding, I would be glad to be with him and if he does go, I want him to come to this company so I can take care of him.*

Two months later, however, Napoleon, feeling honorbound to do his part, joined Co.K of the 36th Regiment of Georgia Volunteers. Moten joined at the same time and was in the same regiment, so that he could look after Napoleon if he should get sick. Their regiment became part of the Army of Tennessee, and they were sent to Vicksburg, Mississippi. Eli was very disappointed when he heard this and expressed his displeasure to his mother.

*I think Pole has done very wrong in leaving home for he will not be apt to be much service in the army on account of his health while he might a done so much good at home, for we all know that we must eat as well as fight and they could not compel him to go. But I reckon he felt it his duty to go, but before twelve months is passed he will wish that he had a took my advice for I begged him in all my last letters to not go and told him how it was and now he has put his head in the halter!*

True to Eli's prediction, Napoleon was taken sick soon after his enlistment because in Eli's letter to him written in July of 1862, he speaks as if he had been home already and should not be in a hurry to return to camp:

*Pole, since a reflection on the matter, I think you acted in a very generous part in going to the War. You have now shown a good will but my advice to you is not to go back to camp too soon for if the fare is as rough in your part as it is here, it is no place for a sick man.*

The very next week, Eli again wrote to his mother to beg

her to get Napoleon to put in for a discharge. He said, "Tell him to get off if he can for there is men getting off much stouter than him."

One of the few letters that have been found from Napoleon to his mother gives some idea of the privations and hardships he had to endure:

*Monday the 5th  Vicksburg Miss*
*My Dear Mother,*
*I take my pen in hand to let you know how I am getting on. I ain't well but I hope these lines may find you well and Bets and the Children well. I ain't got much to write only hard times. I have to buy nearly all I eat or do without. I hain't drawed only three quarters of a pound of meat in ten days. You know that is high living! I took that march to meet our men, but the Yankees had whipt them before we got there. We met them on the retreat. The Yankees had four to our one in the fight and run us thirty miles but we have run them back over the big Black River twenty five miles. I think we will have a fight here yet. They want to enslave us at Jackson but we have been reinforced till I think we can whip them if they fight us on land. I want the fight to come on if it has to come. I want to leave here but it is so hilly we can't hardly travel. It is enough to kill men to travel over the hills. The men is dying here fast. They can't live on the wind and drink wiggletails. Tell all the men to come and help us fight this but tell them to quit fighting for we can't fight no more. I am writing now with a gnawing stomach. I want to go out and get me some milk but the pore men goes four and five miles and pays four dollars a gallon for milk and one dollar for little cabbages. Get six shallots for a dollar and the meal we draw is so coarse till it won't stick together like we like it. The war can't last long I don't think. I want to see the end of it and get home one more time and see you all. Mamma, I can see your pour old withered face jest as plain as I did that morning I left home when I told you goodby for the last time. I have seen H.D. Landers. He has been in the hospital for six weeks. I did not know it till he got well enough to come to see me. He was so glad to see me. He looks bad. We went off to ourselves and talked all day. I went with him to the hospital*

*where he stayed. He got good fare and a good bed to lie on.there
but he come back and stayed all night with me. Dave went back
to his regiment. Mammy I often think since I left you that you
have been the best mother in the world. I want you to write to
me every week. It is a great pleasure to hear from you. Write
and give me all the nuse and go down and see Sarah and Add
and Dan's folks and write how they are coming. They won't
write to me. I have wrote fourteen letters to you all and got two
back. One from you Mamma and one from Sarah. Write soon.
This may be the last time you will hear from me in this life so
farewell my dear Mother. Remember me in this life.*
N.B.Landers to Susan Landers

Soon after this letter was written, Napoleon was put in
a convalescent camp at Morristown. Eli mentioned it in a letter
to his mother:

*I received a letter W.R.sent to R.N. that stated he and
Napoleon was at Moristown at the Convalescent Camp. W.R.
said that it would take close attention to ever raise him. It is
surprising how they will keep men in service that is not able
to wait on theirselves nor never will be. Give N.B. my love in
your next letter. I would write to him but I can't get paper and
stamps for there's none to be had.*

The last letter from Napoleon was written to his
cousin W.M. McDaniel, dated *April 23rd, 1863 from
Vicksburg:*

*Dear Cousin,*
*I take my pen in hand to let you know how I am getting on. I
ain't well nor hast bin for a week but I hope these lines will
come safe to hand and find you all well. I hain't got much to
write. The Yankees passes with the gunboats every day. Before
long we will leave here. I think we will go to Mobile but I don't
know when we will go. The health in the army here is bad. The
men die here fast if you call eight hundred deaths in Vicksburg
bad. All day they are sent to the hospital. We can't live on what
we draw. The meat we draw is spoilt and the beef is so pore we*

131

Napoleon Bonaparte Landers

Adeline and Caroline Landers

Eli wrote his mother from Chickamauga the following words: "It is unknown who will get killed in this fight. It may be me, and if I do get killed, if there is any chance, I want my body taken up and laid in the dust round old Sweetwater and I want a tombstone put at my head with my name and my Co. and Regiment, the day I enlisted and the name and date of all the battles I have ever been in....This is my request if it is possible." Probably due to the hard circumstances in Georgia following the war this request was not realized, and a simple stone marker was put in place. The author discovered this marker (shown at left) in 1990. In September of that year a new headstone was erected, in accordance with Eli Lander's wishes, provided by the 9th Georgia Re-enactment Group. Shown below at the dedication ceremony are, front row, l-r, Pat Price, David Neel, Darly Masters, John Weaver, Cary Medows, and Jimmy Dodd. In the back row are Elizabeth Roberson(the author), Bob Mekon, Carl Whitaker, Darrick Roberson, Stan Neel, Mike Price, Gary Wehner, Fred Langford, Bill Rockwell, James Boyd, Jim Nicholson, Ralph Moyher, David Meyer, Tony Dooley and Tommy Boyd.

*can't eat it. A man can't live here without he spends two dollars a day. I think we will have to give it up and come home. Our men look so pore and bad. The men went to the Brigade wagons to see what they had. Some sell shallots and eggs. They sold um one dollar for six shallots, two dollars for eggs, one dollar for meat. I was so weak they got there first and got all of them Tell Mamma that I don't feel like I will ever see her face again. There is no chance to come home from here. The men dies right and left in front and rear. I pay out from one to two dollars a day and then go hungry. I'm not able to run about and hunt it up. I have got only one letter since I left home. Tell them to write to me or I won't write to them. I have wrote up half a quire of paper to them and haven't got no answer from it. Paper is buyed here when we can get it. Tell Sarah that I think she might write to me. Tell Dan Miner I have rote to him three letters and I want him to rite to me so I must come to a close.*

*N.B.Landers to W.M. McDaniel*

The official records state that Napoleon Landers was captured at Vicksburg, Mississippi on July 4, 1863. He was sick at the time of his capture, and while being moved by boat to a military prison, he died on July 28th,1863 of disease, somewhere between New Orleans and Mobile.

Eli's brother-in-law,Moten, was also taken sick in the summer of 1862, but was able to get home before he died. Soon after Moten's death, his brother,Thomas,wrote to his widow, Adaline, describing the difficult time they had in transporting him home:

*Camp Haten Tennessee July the 14th 1862*
*Dear Sister,*

*It is that I drop you a few lines that leaves me well at present hoping this will come safe and find you and little Henry well and also your mother's folks. I received your letter dated the 9th July yesterday and was glad to hear from you. I regret Brother Moten's death very much as he was the only brother I had left in Gwinnett. He wasn't to have been sent home from Chattanooga but he was carried to Moristown and back to Knoxville before he was sent home. That kept him in camp too long but it was not as I or the Captain pleases about sending him home. I was glad we got the chance to send him home as soon as we did as we could not send him no sooner. I would have went home with him if I could but there was no chance for that so I expect he fared badly on the road home through I am as well contented about the treatment and attention he received after he got home as if I had been there though I had rather been with him if I could. Not that I think I could a nursed him any better than you did but you know it is human nature for anybody to be with their folks in their last hours. This you know by your own feelings without me saying anything about it.*

*Adaline, as for the burial care I suppose you had it fixed to your own notions. I write to let you know I am satisfied with all you have done about it. I merely write this to you so you needn't be afraid of me thinking hard of you in any way you have managed the care for I am satisfied with it as it could not be hoped for death is sure and life uncertain so I reckon I am as well composed as the care will admit. You stated that you thought he was in Heaven. That gave me some consolation. Write how you get along and if you need any money. So I remain your brother, Thomas Hutchins*

Another letter to Adaline from Thomas was written on August 1st, 1862. In it he tries to help her decide what to do about Moten's grave:

*Adaline, I drop you a few lines that leaves me well hoping this will find you and little Henry well. I have nothing interesting to write you. I received your letter of the 16th and was glad to hear from you. I wrote to you some time ago. You said you wanted to get a tombstone for Moten's grave. I would like for it to be done but I think it will be best to let it alone for a while yet until we can see better what can be done. Though you can use your own pleasure about it. I will be satisfied with anything you see proper to do about it but as times is hard and likely to remain so for sometime yet I think it best to let it remain as it is for maybe I may get a chance to come home someday or other but I fear not soon, if ever I do get home. You say if I get sick come and you will wait on me. I will be glad of that. You wrote that Mr. A.D. Jackson said if I get sick he will come after me and that he will do it if I call on him. You wrote like you thought that he would take the advantage of me. If he wants to come for me you need not be afraid of that. I am not afraid to trust myself with him, in that case, for I know him as well as anybody. You said my watch was gone but I have got it. Moten gave it to me before we started. Write to me again. Give all the news so I must close.*

*Your truly brother Thomas Hutchin*
[Author's note: Records show that Moten was buried in the Sweetwater Churchyard, but since there is no stone marking his grave, the family was probably unable to put a headstone there for him.]

Eli had heard of Moten's death while he was in Virginia and had written at that time:

*"I was sorry to hear about Moten's death. It made me feel so bad to read Add's few lines that she thought he would get well but her hope was in vain but we know not what minute we will go the same way for death is certain and life uncertain."*

In just a few short months, Adaline would face another heartache when in November, her little boy, William Henry, died. Eli had been so fond of the child and was saddened by the news of his death:

*I was sorry indeed to hear of dear little Henry's death for I always doted so much on him. I could not keep from shedding tears when I read Caroline's letter about him the way he done before he died. No doubt but the poor little fellow was apprised of his death. He always seemed to be so sensible of everything.*

Sometime within the next year, Adaline married Crockett Rowden, who was from the same county. There have been stories handed down in the family about the strength she had in providing for the family there at home. When she heard that

Sherman and his troops were moving toward them from Atlanta, she hid as much food as possible under the pulpit of the Sweetwater Church, and hung the few hams they had left, under the bridge near their house. The Federal troops passed through unaware that the food was so close by. Thus the family was saved from starving.

Crockett Rowden survived the war and he and Adaline lived there near the Sweetwater Church, where they raised their two daughters, Savannah and Alma.

Eli's half brother, Humphrey Davis Landers, was living in Alabama when the war started. He was married to Wealthy Fowler and had several children, one of whom was Humphrey Davis III, whom Eli called "Little H.D." Even though Humphrey and Eli were only half brothers, they were very devoted to one another as this letter from Humphrey to Eli indicates:

> *Dear Eli,*
> *I have not forgotten you nor never will while I live in this world. I feel very sad this morning. I feel like if I was only with you I would be the happiest person in the world. You are the only single brother I have got and I think more of you than any of the rest. You don't know how proud we was when we read your letter because we thought you were dead!*

Soon after Napoleon enlisted in the army, Humphrey joined Company G of the 30th Alabama Infantry, which was part of the Army of the Tennessee. While serving in the western theatre, he was captured on May 16, 1863 in the battle of Champion Hill, Mississippi, near Baker's Creek. He was then sent to a federal prison in Memphis, Tennessee. On July 4, 1863, he was paroled at Camp Lee, Virginia and allowed to rejoin his regiment in Alabama. Unfortunately, he was captured again on December 16, 1864 at Nashville, Tennessee. From there he was transferred to Camp Douglas, Illinois where he remained in prison until the end of the war.

After his release from prison in June 1865, he returned to Randolph County, Alabama where he applied for a pension in 1908. The pension examiner stated that at that time, he was very feeble with a maimed foot which was the result of an injury he received while in the war. He was said to be quite stooped and had to walk with both hands on a long stick. Due to his debilitated condition, he was given a pension. Humphrey died in 1913 and was buried at the Corinth Baptist Church cemetery in Randolph County. His son, "Little H.D.", grew up to become the chief clerk in the office of the Probate Judge. He also served as a school teacher, lawyer, and justice of the Peace for Randolph County. His wife, Mary Ann Ayers, was the local postmistress, and conducted the postal service out of their home, known as "Wildwood." H.D. died in 1940 and was buried next to his father at Corinth Church. All of their ten children carried on the tradition of the love of learning that Eli possessed, as seven of them became teachers or principals of schools in Alabama.

Eli's sister, Elizabeth, whose husband, Willard Pinckney Mason, was killed in 1862, married Sam Dyer, a good friend of the family. He had enlisted with Eli, but served in the 3rd Battalion of Georgia Sharpshooters. He was captured just two months before the end of the war and was released from prison at Point Lookout, Maryland in June 1865. After the war, he and Elizabeth continued to live in Gwinnett County.

Caroline married J.J. Arnold in 1864. Apparently he died soon after that, and then it appears that she re-married. According to information written on the back of a photograph of Caroline which was taken in her later years, her last name was Norman, and she was living in Biloxi, Mississippi.

Harriet, whose husband, Daniel Miner, was killed in 1863, never re-married, but continued to live there in Gwinnett County. Her son, Eli Pinson, was named after his uncle.

Eli's cousin, Elijah Moore McDaniel, with whom he served in the Sixteenth Regiment, was captured at Cold Harbor, Virginia in June, 1864 and was released from prison at Elmira, New York in June 1865. He returned home to Gwinnett County and married Mary F. Massey. He became very active in the community and was a leader in the political affairs of the county. His brother, Archibald, whom Eli referred to as "Arch", also survived the war and died in 1888.

Another cousin, W.M. McDaniel, was captured at Cold Harbor at the same time of E.M.'s capture, but he died of smallpox at the Elmira Prison only two days before he was to be released. He is buried in Woodlawn National Cemetery.

As for Eli's beloved mother, Susan, there is little record of what happened to her after the devastation of war took the lives of so many of her family. A notation in the family bible states that she died on September 25th, 1883. In memoirs written by her stepson, Humphrey Davis, she was buried in the graveyard at Sweetwater Church. No stone exists to show the exact location. A visitor to that cemetery however, will see a grave beside Eli's that has no marker. This is perhaps Susan Landers' resting place. If so, mother and son, separated in life by war, lie together now in death.

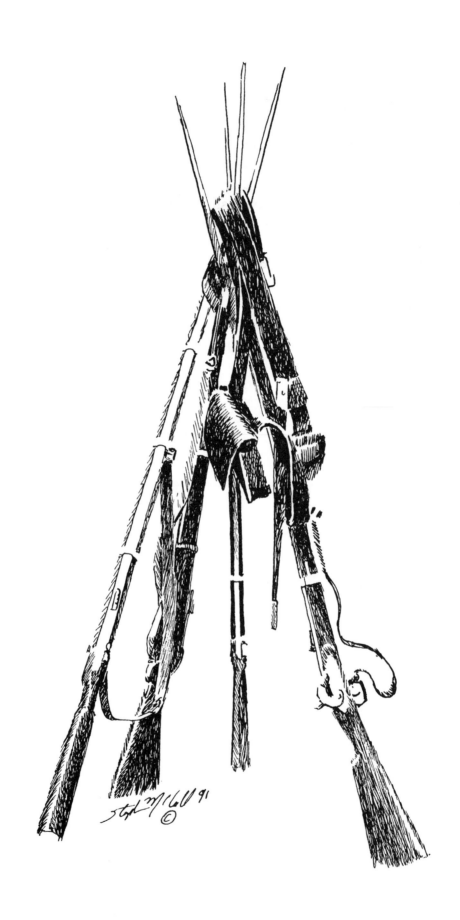

## *Appendix II*
## *Other Letters of*
## *Eli Pinson Landers*

Richmond  Sept 21st 1861

My dear Sister Caroline

      I will write you a few lines with much gratification from your short words to me. These lines leaves me well and hearty and trusting that they may find you well. I am in a poor condition for writing this evening but I will write some anyway. I would like to see you the best in the world. I just want to tell you all about the fun. Car I want you to write to me and write about everybody and everything for I love to read your letters. Car if I never see you again let wisdom be your guide and recollect that I am your friend and well wishes. Remember that you had a brother that laid down his life for your honorable rights.  Let Patriotism encourage your feelings. Live a prudent and moral life for if we go down to Yorktown and get into a difficulty with the Yankeys they may tug me. Car Bill is just got well of the measels and he says for you to keep his fiddle till he comes home. Car tell Miss Jane that I love her yet.  Give my best respects to all the girls and tell them that I have not forgot none of them. Tell Paulina that I look at the left side of my coat and think of her. The sewing has not ripped yet. give my respects to Pole and Sarah. Tell Sarah that Dave has been sick  nearly ever since he has been here with his head but he is getting well. Give my entire respects to Elizabeth and Harriet and their family. Give my best love to all Unkle Eli's family and to James Garner and tell him that I wish that I could be there to help him to dam up his dam again but he will have to get it done without me. So I must close for the want of time.

      Round is the ring that has no end. I send my love to you my friend.
      E.P.Landers to his sister H.C.Landers

Note: The sewing on Eli's coat as mentioned in the letter was probably referring to some kind of "name tag" that was sewn on a soldier's coat in the event of his being killed on the battlefield and there being no one there to identify the body.

*Weep Not for Me Dear Mother*

To Moten and Ad and Henry

My dear friends, I will send a word to you. Ad you don't know my feelings towards you all. We will leave this place in a few days but I don't much care for I am bedeviled nearly to death so that I don't care how soon we fight it out. Moten, I can only say howda to you. That is with as gooder feeling towards you as if I had writ a whole column. But the drum is beating for drill and everybody has to steer. Moten I would like to see you very well. Say howda to little William Henry. I want to see you so bad that I don't know what to do. I want you to write soon as you get this for I want to hear from you all before I leave this place for I may not hear from you any more for the Yankeys is as thick as hops down about where we are going. I will send this letter by Mr. Hutchins to Yellow River. I am in such a hurry that you must excuse my bad writing. Tell John W. Shamblee that I saw Nick the other day. He is getting well. He talks like getting a furlough to come home on when he gets able to travel. So I must close for this time. Write soon. I'd like to see William Henry walking. Tell him to not stump his toes. So no more only remaining your brother as ever.

E.P.Landers for the War. Goodby

Richmond  Septs 21st 1861

My Honored Mother

With pleasure I resume my seat to write you a few lines to let you know that I am well at this time truly hoping that these few lines may find you all well. W.P.Mason received a letter from Liz this morning. We was glad to hear from you. I have nothing new to write. Times is very good here with plenty to eat and nothing to do but we are looking everyday when we will get the job. We are still at Richmond but we are looking every day when we will start to Yorktown. The Vice President made us a speach the other evening. He said that he would insure us to be well armed in the course of the next week then we will march immediately but I feel willing to go. I have just laid around here like Brutus till I don't care for little things. Mamma it has been some time since I received a word of consolation from you only them few words which Car sent in Pinks letter. It made me think a heap of her. I want you when one of you write for all of you to put in a word. I want you to write as soon as you get this. Don't wait. Write if you ever got that ambertype I sent by Mr. John Mills and write if you think it favors me or not and if N.B. has got my old one or not and tell him that he owes me a letter for it and I shall look for it to come.

I want you to write if you got them two dollars that I sent or not and write everything that you know. Write a long satisfactory letter and if you can't send it in one letter send it in two. Tell all to write.

I dream about you all nearly every night. I drempt Mamma had come to see me and I was going about over Richmond with you but I hope that the day will come when it will not be in dreams that I will be with you when we will set down round your table to eat in independent peace for that is the only way that I ever expect to eat with you again.

My dear Mother this is a dreadful life but I feel reconciled to it for I believe that we are on the right side of the question. They brought in 2000 more Yankeys the other day but that is nothing for there is more prisoners in Richmond now than they know what to do with. Mamma save all the fodder and hay that you can for I want you to keep my filly if you can possibly do it for if we whip the devils and I get back home I will need her. Jo Waldrop has gone home. He started this morning. He got a discharge. W.T.Smith is most well. One of the Lawrenceville boys died this morning. His name was Kemp. There has four died out of our Co.

Mamma, I think about you every hour in the day. I just think about you working so hard without me till I hardly can stand it. It was hard enough when I was there to help you but you must do the best you can. It is hard for you to do without me and for me to lie on my blanket but I freely do it for my freedom Tell all my connections howda for me and all the girls. Tell Miss Juley and Miss Margret Hopkins howda for me and tell them I thank them for their compliments to me so Mamma well wishes to you. I must close Farewell my dearest friend. so no more only remaining yours truly.

E.P.Landers to Susan Landers at home

Richmond VA  Oct the 14th 1861

Dear Brother,

I received your letter last night and was proud to hear from you all and to hear that all was well but Mamma. I was very sorry to hear that Mamma had got her arm broken. It is a pity but I hope that the neighbors will attend to her farm till she can use her arm again. Pole, this letter leaves me a little better than I was yesterday though I did not rest as good last night as I did the night before. I sent for the doctor last night but he did not come. He will be here this morning for sure. I hope that I will not have a spell of the fever if I can get the doctor here in time to break it up before it goes too far. Pole I am at a private house and the people is as clever to me as if I was a kin to them. I am on a feather bed and as many pillows as I want. Arch stayed with me last night. He waited on me like I was his brother but that still aint like it was Mamma but I am well satisfied considering everything.

The report is that we will get our guns today and leave here Wednesday for Yorktown but I don't know whether it is so or not for there is many reports in camp that I don't know when to believe anything. If the Regiment leaves this week I will not be able to go with the boys. I will keep Arch to wait on me if I can for I rather him or Lige would wait on me as anybody else. The Captain will detail him to stay with me if it is in his power to do so. Tell Mamma to not be uneasy about me for I get the best kind of attention from the people that I am staying with and the Capt does all he can for me by sending the boys out to wait on me. The lady of the house put a mustard plaster on my back. I let it stay till it burnt it well and it hope me. Tell Mamma to take good care of her arm and let it get well as soon as possible for she is the dependance and not study about me. Pole I want to see you mity bad but Pole I advise you as a brother to stay at home and take care of your money for I know that money is hard to get in Gwinnett. It will cost you not less than forty five dollars to come and go and that is a heap of money for you to dig out of the ground. Pole keep your money for the use of your family and for Mamma for I know that she is needy. I want you to write to me often. Pink is well. He nearly cried when I read about little Charles. I must close hoping this will find you all well and will write to me soon.

E.P.Landers and A.W.McDaniel to Brother Daniel

I want to say something to you. Me and Brother is well and very well satisfied though we want to see you all mity bad. Dave Cruse is getting well of the mumps but won't be able for service under two weeks. Brother Daniel, I don't want you to volunteer in none of them twelve months companys for it would break Pap up if he could not make a living for his helpless family of children. Brother, do all you can for to keep them from suffering. I don't mean just for something to eat but be as saving as possible for it will take nearly all the money that you all make to pay taxes and I expect that you and Pap will have to borrow money to pay them. I must close. Give my respects to all our folks and to all my friends and relations.
     Your Brother  A.W.McDaniel

Richmond Va  Oct 25th 1861

My Dear Mother
          Today I am going to try to write you a letter to let you know how I am. I am getting better. I can walk about in the house now. I have been sick nearly 3 weeks. I was taken with the intermittent fever and I was just getting well of that when I was taken with the measels but they did not hurt me much. My Regiment has left me and gone to Yorktown. They left last Saturday morning about day. The doctors would not let nobody stay with me but I have done very well without them. I reckon that I will go to camp in 3 or 4 weeks if I don't get no backset for I want to be sound when I try it again for I will tell you the camp is a rough place. I would like to see some of you but I reckon there is no chance for money is so scarce. I would get a furlough and come home but there can be no furlough got now. I want you to write as soon as you get this letter and just what you sent by R.B. Martin for I have never got nothing yet. Asa Wright said that there was a box of things that Mr. Mason brought. He did not know wheather there was anything in it for me or not but he said that there was a coverlid on the top

of it. I allowed it was for me. Tell Pole I want to see him mighty bad. Give my love to all for I can't separate them.

I am staying with Mr. Pemberton. They treat me as well as they can they tend to me like I was a child though I have to pay my way and I have not got the money to pay them now but they say to not mind that for if I didn't have a cent they would treat me as well as if I had 1000 dollars. They have took in about 70 solgers since the war began. Mamma don't be uneasy about me for I will do the best I can for myself. Direct your letter to me. Don't have it in care of the Capt. If you do it will go right on to the Co before I get it. Dave Haney is at the St.Charles Hospital. Us two is all that was left. N.Shamblee is at the same place yet. I am now sitting and I have sot longer this time than I ever have before. I think all I need now is to take good care of myself and have something to eat which I get plenty of and that is good. W.D. Cruse went off with mumps or he was not well of them. There is 6 Negroes here that wait on me well. No white folks only the old man and woman. I was sorry to hear of you getting your arm broke but I hope it will do well so I must close for I feel so tired. Write just as soon as you get this for I want to hear from you. I have thought of you often since I have been sick but thoughts was all. Tell Car howda so no more at present only I remains your son as ever. So goodby for this time.

E.P.Landers to Susan Landers

November 4th 1861

My Dear Child,

I feel like if I can't be with you I wish to speak in the way of lines. This leaves all well. My arm is mending fast. I hope this may find you mending too. We started a letter to you by Ely and he got as far as Atlanta and he give out but he's going again next Monday. And you said for me to write you as soon as I got your letter. I was mighty glad to hear you was getting better. I sent you a little by Paiden and I wish to know if you received them or not. Ely took the box to Atlanta and left them. We sent you a butter coverlid and a pair of pants, potatoes, sweetbread and a half quire of paper. He will take them Monday. I reckon there weren't anything in W.J. Morons box for you. That coverlid was Pink's. We would of sent your things by Rito but we heard he was not allowed to take no box. I was very sorry to hear they would not let no person stay with you. But you said you got good attention from the people you stay with. Give Mr and Mrs Pemberton my humble thanks. I hope the Lord will reward them for it. You said you was scarce of money and I expect it will take all you draw to pay your way and if you cannot make out when you go back to your company I will send you some if I can sell my mule. But be sure and don't go back to your company too soon if you remain weakly. Ely says he is going to bring you home. If I had the money I would come but he expects to stay there 2 or 3 weeks. I would write more but it is Monday morning and I have to send Caroline to the post office and Ely could not get off last Friday with your letter..

I do want to see you mighty bad and talk with you. But my child take good care of yourself and don't go to camp too soon. I hope the Lord will be your friend for he is all our dependance. Look to Him for help. I want to know if you have thought of those things. I do crave to see your pleasant face. I will close. Goodby if I never see you no more write soon and often to me. I could read letters from you all day. Moten hasn't moved yet. We will give you more satisfaction the next time.

Susan Landers to E.P.Landers

Richmond VA  Nov 15th 1861

My Dear Mother,

This morning I will drop you a few lines to let you know how I am. I am not as well as I was when I wrote my last letter since that time I have had a disease nearly like the mumps. It got in my secrets an I thought that I would be ruined. I suffered tremendously though I am now getting over that. I have had a hard time of it. I don't no when I will go back to camp. the Capt sent me word by old man Franklin to stay in Richmond till I got perfectly well for he says where they are there is no place for a sick man. They say it is a very cold wet part of the world. I don't believe that I will be able to stand the camps this winter for they are exposed and sent out on picket two or three miles from the camp on the bank of the waters where the wind can come from a long ways off. The picket says that sometimes they can see the Yankey vessels sailing about away off from the shore. They just can discover them that they are throwing up breastworks.

Bill Elis is here now. He is coming home. He is discharged and sais it is tuff times. He sais that it takes nearly all of the well solgers for duty. Nun hardly to drill. They have some for picket guard and some to guard round the Regiment and some to work at the breastworks. So I don't think that I can stand it for it is so cold and most always rainy. Bad weather. I have bin here 5 weeks today. I now owe Mr. Pemberton 20 dollars. I will tell you that it is taking a pore man's pocket change tolerable low. I have not got but 5 dollars and 50 cts in my pocket though I recon that I will draw my wages. I am not near as well as I was two weeks ago. I don't no what I will do for I don't want to go to a hospital for I had nearly as well be in camp but I don't think that Mr. Pemberton will be particular about the money for he's a mighty fine old man. I think that they ought to give me a discharge but they say that a man must have some settled disease. But I am not able for survice. I have bin looking for Unkle Ely for the last two days. You said he would start Monday and this is Friday an he has not come yet. Last night I was the worst fooled. In the night I herd somebody come to the outside door and called me to unlock the door. the voice was just like Unkle Ely. I jumped up and opened my room door and unlocked the door and was fixing to shake hands with him and when he stepped in it was one of the boarders that had just bin out in town and was just coming in. I was mad. Mamma don't you be uneasy about me for I have got as much sense as I ever had but that's not much. I will try to take care of myself the best I can and I have a few friends in Va yet if I can just get my health and keep it things will be alright with me. I hate to hear of you and Car being so troubled about me. It is true that I have bin through the rubs but I hope for better times to come. I would like to be at home to stay till I get well but ther is no more furloughs to be given tell after the 4th of January. They have very tight laws in the army. Maw try to reconcile yourself about me for you can't mend the matter. Tell Pole I wish I could see his crop of corn. There is good crops in Va. Corn is from 55 to 60 cts. Tell Pole that down about Bethel close by Yorktown the Yankeys took possession of a settlement of corn and thought they was doing big things and old General Magruder went an run them off and is now a gathering the corn. He has gathered 500 wagon loads. I wish that the President would send us to Savannah where the weather would be warmer and we would be closer home. Times is hard in Richmond. Salt is 25 dollars a sack, beef 12 and a half cts per pound, chickens 30 cts.,butter 40 cts.

I got a letter from Yorktown the time I got yours. Arch and Lige had the mumps and they was in a bad fix. They was in and out of a house and Dave Cruse is waiting on them. It is a good tight house. If If go to camp and get sick I think I will go to that house and not have to pay so much. They can get good fare in there and be comfortable. Elis sais that they are most well now. Give my love to all the connections and to all inquiring friends. Tell them to write. Tell them I am a man now. I will weigh fully a 100 lbs. Tell Pole that somebody stoled my brandy. Spirits is very high at Yorktown. You have to pay 25 cts. a drink and one dollar 25 cts a qt. for brandy. That is very hi drinking. If a man had 500 gallons of peach brandy there or up on the Potomac he could make a fortune of it. Well I will close. Write soon and write how full the corn crib is and how you are managing the hogs and if you have got any pigs and if my sow has ever had any pigs. I want to no all about what is going on so good by till I hear from you again.

E.P.Landers to Susan


Moten and Adaline, I will write some to you too. I got your letter that you sent by Peden. You all had better send me a pocket full of letters by him.again. It took me an hour to read them. I would like to see you all the best kind but I will tell you I am under the tight rules of Jeff Davis. I am mighty weak and no account. I don't no wheather I will get through the winter or not. Tell little William Henry to make them open the trunk when ever he wants. I sent him 3 cts. by Asa Wright. Tell him to shake it at the other little boys and tell them rich folks will be rich. Moten I want you to move as soon as you can for I will be better satisfied if you was down there. I have bin sick 6 weeks and have bin here 5 weeks today and no money and not well yet and I am afraid that when I do get well I am afraid that being exposed as the poor solgers has to be I am afraid that I will not get through the winter. So I must close for the want of room. It is cold and cloudy now. Write soon.

Moten, I wouldn't let your horse go for you will need it but try to sell the mule if it will sell at all. so no more for this time. I could tell you a heap but I can't write much more.

E.P.Landers to Moten and Adaline Huchins

Camp near Richmond Va  May 29th  1862

Dear Mother and Lonely Sisters,

　　　I your son and brother takes pleasure this morning in writing to you to let you know that I am yet in the land of the living. But not to say right well. I have got the jaw ache though it don't pain me any today. I hope that this may find you all well and in good health for that is the greatest blessing that we enjoy. It has been some time since I heard from you by letter but I understand that N.B. has gone to the War and I feel very anxious to hear from you to know how you are making out by yourselves. Though I know it is a bad time with you all I think that N.B. has done very wrong in leaving home for he will not be apt to be much service in the army on account of his health while he might a done so much good at home for we all know that we must eat as well as fight and they could not compel him to go. But I reckon that he felt it his duty to go but before 12 months he will wish that he had a took my advice for I begged him in all my last letters to not go and told him how it was and now he has put his head in the halter. He will have to do the best he can but being as he intended to go I had rather than l00 dollars that he had a come to this Co. I can't hear nothing from Moten whether he is gone or not. I have been very much disatisfied ever since I heard that N.B. was gone for I don't know what you will do for I reckon that Moten will have to go but you must do the best you can and get shet of some of your stock and don't try to tend too much land. Tend the best spots and you will make more than to try to tend all and if you can't feed her I reckon you will have to sell my mare but I hate mitely to part with her but you must do what you think best for I don't want you to keep her and suffer on account of it. But keep her if you can and if you sell her be very careful who you sell to for these times there is no telling what man or money is good. Add you and H.C. must be very careful with the horses and the plow or you will have some old runaway scrapes. You had better tend as much bottom land as you can for that is where the corn grows but I reckon that you know your own business best for you are there where you can see what is needed while I am many miles away but my best desire is with you and for you and under the present conditions of affairs I feel it my duty to send my money to you. I did think that I would finish paying Mr. Pemberton but as he is so very wealthy and you so dependent I think it no more than my duty to let what money I can spare go to help support you. I will say no more about that. I haven't anything very interesting to write but we have moved since I wrote to you last. We moved off of the River on the other side of Richmond. We are in about 3 miles of Richmond but I can't get no chance to go to see my old friends. We come through Richmond the other day but we was not allowed to stop. There is great fear of the Yankeys taking Richmond. They are in sight of us with a large force. We are expecting a general engagement every day. It is thought that there will be the hardest fighting around this place that ever has been heard of for the Enemy will do their game fighting to get the city but our men has formed a resolution for the streets to flow with blood before we give it up. There was a fight in hearing of us on the 27th. We could hear their guns plain but we have not heard how it went. I want you to write as soon as you can and tell me all the nuse and if N.B. and Moten is gone. Let me know the number of their regiment and the letter of their company and their P.O. so that I can write to them. Tell them to write to me. Elijah.and Arch is both complaining this morning. Pink is in Richmond yet but is getting well. George W. Atkinson is dead. He died on the 26th. He had his health best of arry man in the Co till a few days before he died. He took the Brain fever. Tell Sq Mc that I saw William Henry yesterday. He is well and in fine spirits. I meet up with more of my old Georgia friends here than if I was in Ga. Please send me some good strong thread and needles for I have lost mine and send me a hat too. So I will close.

    E.P.Landers to Susan Landers

A Camp near Richmond  June 10th  1862

My Dear Mother and Sisters,

    I feel proud that I am permitted to answer another letter from you which came to hand yesterday and as according to your request found me well. This leaves me in good health hoping you may read it in like manner. I have nothing new to write at present but I think that I can afford to reply to all your letters. From the reading of the letters that come to this Co I see that it is reported that I was dead but I feel blest and happy to inform you that it it is not the case. I have received them things sent by Cain and they come in a good time for I was nearly bareheaded and the next day was a wet day. I see now what a great advantage it is to have friends to provide when a person has no chance to help themselves. But it looks like if you can provide for yourself that I need not be uneasy about myself. It makes me feel bad when I think how hard you have to struggle for a support in your old days but we all see how it is for we know there is no other chance till the word is given peace and I fear that will not be soon but oh may the time speedily come when I will have the privilege of enjoying the comforts and pleasure of my old peaceful home where I spent so many days of pleasure and not knowing how to appreciate it. But that time has passed not to return. Mr. Liddell came to camp yesterday and I was glad to see him for I knew I would hear from home. Well H.C. you wanted to know what we get to eat. We get meat and bread. Sometimes we get enough and sometimes we don't but we have not suffered bad since we come to Richmond. We don't get hardly any salt. That is the worst difficulty but on a march we don't get much but this morning we had one of the best messes of bacon dumplings out of jail. We have bought right smart of little extras to eat but had to pay so high for them till our money has give out and we hant drawed any yet nor I don't no when we will. It looks like they never will pay me. I am due over 100$ in wages but this is the first time I have ever been without money yet. But I am not by myself for nearly all the Co is in the same fix. But we will all do the best we can. We haven't got no tents nor don't want none till winter time. Mamma you said that you did not think that I ever would read your letter but you must not think that I am killed everytime you hear of a battle. It is true I am just as liable as any person but I have been spared till now. I was close by the fight but was not engaged. I could hear them but did not see them. It was a very hard struggle indeed lasting 8 hours hard fighting. The loss was very heavy on each side. Our loss was about 3000 but greater on the other hand. We drove them off the field taking many prisoners. We don't know when we will try it again. We have moved about 1 mile from the place I wrote before of the picket line to rest Just one Co has to go on picket at a time so we will get to rest. I don't want you to be so uneasy about me for I will try to do the best I can. Liz I am glad you thought to write to me. I would be glad to reply it individually but you may consider yourself included in this. Tell the little boys they must quit fighting. I would like to see them take a twist. Tell Margaret I ain't told her Pa yet. Give my entire love and respects to Ad and Harriet and family and to all inquiring friends and especially to the fair ladies of Sweetwater. Well Mamma I don't know what is best for you to do with my mare for I am afraid that she will be ruined if she is not used some and I won't want to take less than she is worth and I don't know what to say but if you keep her try to get some old sturdy man to plow her a few days but don't let her out all the time. Mamma a few words concerning yourn and Sarahs affairs about living together. You had better live separate. You know it will be best for you both. You must not work too hard for you can't hold out at it. It would be a pleasure to me to run round your young corn patch in the upper bottom but instead of coming towards home there is a great talk of us having to go to Maryland to reinforce General Jackson but we don't know for certain. I told you that I had nothing to write and I reckon you will see its true. Send my respects to Moten and N.B. in your letters. Tell them to let me know who is in their mess. This is a rainy wet day and looks like it will rain all night but me and E.M. and A.W. has got a blanket stretched till it don't leak much so with my best respects to you all I will bring my letter to a close by saying I remain your affectionate son and brother as ever and by requesting you to write when you can hoping that the time will soon come when I will see you again but if you on earth I never see, in all your prayers remember me.

E.P. Landers to his Mother Susan Landers at home

Mamma your ambertype is in Petersburg in the Captain's trunk.

Camp near Winchester  Oct l7th 1862
My Dear Mother,

        I am favored with the opportunity of answering another letter from you which I received yesterday morning and was glad indeed to hear from you all. I am well this morning but as for nuse I have nothing new more than we are expecting another fight now very soon at Charlestown about l5 miles from here. The Enemy made an attempt to advance yesterday and I suppose they taken Charlestown and we had orders last night to cook up rations and be ready to leave at any minute though we did not leave last night. But we are now packed up and ready to start and expecting orders every minute. I don't know which way we will go to meet the Enemy and some thinks we will fall back towards Staunton but it is my opinion that we will meet the Enemy and if we do we will have warm times. Our regiment has not increased very much for the last month men coming in from the hospital and a good many conscripts has joined us. There is some sickness in camp at this time. There is a good many cases of the smallpox with us but there has not been but 2 cases in our regiment yet though it was reported yesterday that nearly all of the 7th Ga Regt had them. I am afraid that they will ruin our army if they get started. I wrote you a letter the other day and I have no nuse to write today. I merely write in answer to yours and I felt somewhat interested in one part of your letter though I don't know what to say. That is about your arrangements for another year. I have conversed with S.E. Massey about him and he knows all about him. He says that he will not do no good without an overseer and that you know he will not have that and he says that he will ruin my filly. I think they you had better both come under close obligations of writings and have them witnessed by competent men so that he can't falter from the bargain. Give him no advantage for he will take enough anyhow. I wrote the other day for you to be careful who you got but I suppose times is so that a person can't get just anybody. But he has got too many in the family though he may be better than he is represented. I would let Unkle Eli see to matters ever once in a while and one thing I want you to tell him to be very careful with my filly for I would not have her spoilt in breaking for all he would make. For fear you will not get my last letter I will tell you in this if I was you I would rent N.B.'s upper field and have it sowed in wheat. A few words to Unkle Eli if you please when Mr. Cofer moves in. I want you to notice ever once in a while and see that he don't get too large for his trousers thinking there is no man to prevent him. I have not heard from the Boys yet but I suppose all of the wounded was sent to Richmond but you have a better chance to get the nuse than we do for we get no papers. I feel very much lost since the Fight. I dream about the boys often. Extend my love through the family and receive your own portion. So all keep in good heart and do the best you can.

Mamma I have drew me a pair of pants and I have got 2 coats and I think I can make out without any from home without there was some certain way to get them. I was glad to hear that you was making enough corn to do you for that is more than many will do. Ma I don't want you to make yourself so uneasy about me for it will do neither of us any good and by the help of God I will try to take care of myself notwithstanding there is many dangers and trials to undergo. But if it be my lot to never return home let us be reconciled.

I was glad to hear from H.D. for I had often wondered where he was though I don't know when I will have the chance to write to him nor N.B. for I don't have the chance to write to anybody but you. But the people must excuse me. I want you to write ever chance for I am always so glad to hear the nuse from my old home. I want to know what has become of N.B.'s horse. Give my love to all the connections and inquiring friends. Tell Harriet and children I have not forgot them. Tell Bill and Nick that they are growing up for such times I am now seeing and to harden themselves for it. Tell Mr. Miner that I have not heard from R.N. since he went to the hospital. Well Mamma, I can't compose my mind to writing this morning. It's roving with you all and on our affairs here so you must overlook all mistakes. Remember my love for you as an affectionate son and well wishes. I hope the day will soon come when I can return to you again.

E.P.Landers Your Devoted Son till Death

Camp near Fredericksburg Va Dec 10th 1862
Dear Mother,

This morning I will write you a few lines to inform you that I am well and I hope this may find you all well. I have nothing new to write as I have just wrote to you the other day. Mr.G.W.Shamblee come in yesterday evening. We was all very glad to see him. He brought everything through safe. I was glad to get my overcoat for I was needing it very bad. It is worth 50 dollars to me for we need everything we can get to keep us warm for the weather is very cold here now. I have been looking for Mr. Shaamblee for some time. I told the boys when he come he would bring me my overcoat with some potatoes in it and when I unfolded it I found my words true. I said I would not take 5 dollars for them. I roasted them last night. Mamma I am at a loss to know what is best to do about clothes. I have got as much as I need all but pants. I have no pants worth anything and if I don't get to draw some before long I will be without any and the quartermaster says that we will not draw anymore clothing money. What we draw from now on will come out of our wages so I will just say to you if you can when E.M. comes back to send me one pair of pants. That is all that I need as for a waistcoat I have got a short coat that will do for that. I don't know whether there will be anymore clothing come in to draw or not. It looks like a heap of trouble to send me so much but I reckon it is the best I can do but I hope it will not be long till I can be at home so they won't have to be sent to me. I am always glad to hear from you. I have had no chance to talk to Mr. Shamblee for he never come till late and then went out to a house last night and hant come back yet but your letter was a heap of satisfaction to me but it makes me feel bad to hear of so many of our friends dying. Mr. Shamblee has come back now and is going to start in a few minutes. I will have to hurry through you must all excuse me for not writing no more. I did aim to write to you all but you see how it is. Mamma you said that you had 10 acres of wheat sowed on your place. I want to know if it is all yours and I want to know what you will do with the fresh field. I just want to know all about it. It does me more good to hear the likes of that than anything else. You wanted to know if any of that fortune teller words was true. As for being sick I was not well for a week. That much was true and I have had plenty of money to do me so that much was true but I put no faith in none of it. Mammy you said you did not have corn to do you. I expect you had better buy some bread corn now for I don't think it will be any cheaper. You said that you aimed to save the money you got for my steers for me. I don't want you to do it if you need it. I don't want you to suffer on my account. I will send you 45 dollars by Mr. Shamblee and ten dollars to Aunt Cebell McDaniel. That is what I got for the boys clothes. Tell Liz that I let Pink have 2 dollars a few days before the fight and I sold them sox of his for one dollar. I will take it in that way or she can take her pay out of this money. Mamma Capt. Reeder let me have 13 dollars last winter when I was sick and I hant never paid him. I want you to pay Mrs. Reeder for me. I think she is the one to pay now. This 5 dollar bill on Hamburg [sic]I have saved it a long time to send to you. It looks like money used to. I will keep about 25 dollars for myself for we have to spend a heap for something to eat or suffer but I think I can do till we draw again. Ma if Mr. Mathews will plow her himself let him work my mare some but I don't want a woman nor boy to fool with her. Ad I would like to reply to your part of the letter but I hant got time but it is as acceptable as if I was to write a week. Give E.M. my best respects. Tell him I want to see him very bad. I don't know what is the reason you did not hear from me for I wrote every 2 weeks. I want you all to write when you can. Give my love to all the family and connections and to all inquiring friends. You write like you thought the war would stop for 4 months. For God's sake don't flatter yourselves with such trash for when it stops for 4 months it will stop for good. If I only had time I could write with more satisfaction but I am hurried so don't hardly know what I am writing. Tell E.M. to bring me a dram when he comes. Return my respects to Miss Mary, Matt and Miss Paulina. Miss P.H. has certainly fell out with me or I would hear from her. Mamma I am well pleased with your arrangements for another year much better than I was with the other. Trade with Cofer. I want you and H.C. if you hant got good winter shoes to get them and let them cost what they may. I have got them you sent to me. Ad I am truly sorry for you. Your lot seems hard so it does but don't be discouraged. Liz, Pink will come home as soon as he gets able. We have not heard from them. We are expecting Lieut. Martin and Asy Wright to return soon. Their time is out. Mr. Shamblee can tell you as much as I can write so I will close for this time. Excuse this sorry letter for its a hurried up one. Give my respects to N.B. Tell Harriet I will present little Ely something the first chance. So nothing more only my love to you all.

E.P. Landers to his Mother Susan Landers at home

*Weep Not for Me Dear Mother*

Fredericksburg VA  Feb 25th 1863
Dear Mother,

This morning I will endeavor to answer your letter that I was so glad to receive for it had been a long time since I heard from you. This will inform you that I am well with the exception of a very bad cold. Mr. Todd got back last Saturday night. He brought everything safe through but my brandy. He drank it up before he got here. Mine and R.N.'s too. But he said he would pay it back the first chance. I was so glad to get my butter that I did not think much about the brandy but he brought 2 bottles of brandy to some of my mess and I got as much of that as done me any good. There is 6 of us and after drinking a half gallon of good old peach we was all rich enough. We had a fine feast for breakfast that morning when Mr. Todd brought John Wallis some sausage meat and me some butter. I tell you it made me think of old times. It did not taste like this old Furkin [sic]Butter we get at $2.50cts a pound. We have got over half of it yet. My shirt come in a good time for I did not have but one. We have had some awful bad weather here of late. Last Sunday was the coldest day I ever saw. I think the snow is now from one to two feet deep. We have had nothing but snow here lately. I have saw more snow this winter than I ever saw in my life. Ma you said that if I needed anything to send for it but I reckon I can make out with what I have got for we can't carry much on a march and we are ordered away from here as soon as the weather gets so we can travel. A large portion of our army has been sent off but I don't know where they got to. But it is thought that we will go down below Petersburg. They are expecting a forward movement on Petersburg soon. I am very willing to leave this place for we have burnt up all the wood around here. We have to burn old field pine bushes or tote our oak wood over a half mile. This part of the country is ruined for all the timber is cut down. Mamma you said that you was afraid that H.C. could not plow Kate. I doubt it myself and if you like him and can get him you had better hire that Mr. Roberts for one month or long as you think best. A good month's work at this time would be worth a heap fixing up the ground to plant. If you hire him keep him at the plow all the time for you and that is the main thing and if he is a trusty fellow I want him to plow my little Jane. I want her worked some if there is any chance. H.C. you said that you was going to ride her. If you are not afraid to ride her I don't care how much you ride her but be very careful that she don't hurt you. If I was there I could trot her Though. I know she is great trouble and expense I am not ready to take what N.B. did for his horse. You said something about paying your debts. I reckon it is a very good idea but keep enough to answer yourself for you may need it and I don't know when they will pay us again. I understand that Congress has raised our wages 5 dollars a month You seem to fear that I rest very uneasy about affairs at home but I reckon that I trouble myself as little about it as any person could for I feel confident that you will all do the best you can and I know everything must work out accordingly and there is no use to study too much about it. I know you all have hard times but I can't help it. It is hard everywhere but I had rather live on dry bread the rest of my life and live in peace than to remain here exposed to so many exposures and dangers. But I expect to serve as long as the Revolutioners if I should live unless honorably discharged sooner for I see the evil of deserters. There has

4 or 5 of this brigade deserted and when they brought them back they looked like they was sent for and could not come. They are now under guard waiting for their trial. Adaline you must take this for an answer to your letter for it is as much to one as another and I have 5 or 6 letters to write as soon as I can. I was very sorry that Bill Smith lost my letter and did not mail it. I thought of it many times. I was surprised when I took it from round the butter and began to read it but it is too late now. The beautiful little damsel is married now. H.C. you said something about a certain long letter but I don't know when that letter will be written for I expect I know as much about something as you do. so I have no more to say. This is a nice warm day. I have sot here and writ till I am getting cold. Tell Arch I received his letter last night. I was glad to hear from him. Give him and all the connections my best love and respects. Give Dan and Harriet my love. Kiss little Ely for me. Give my respects to all inquiring friends and especially to Mr. Thos Matthews. I could write more but I think it is no use. Liz the Capt says your papers is all right and he thinks he can get the money if he can get off to Richmond to file his claims. He says he has writ to see if he can have it tended to in Richmond. If not he will have to go himself and it may be a long time but he will tend to it as soon as he can so I will close with my love to you all.

E.P.Landers to Susan Landers

Camp near Orange C.H. Va    Aug 10 1863
Sunday Morning
Dear Mother.

I read yours of the 30th a few minutes ago. I was glad to hear from you. All this will inform you that I am well and hearty. I have nothing new to write as I just wrote you the other day. Nothing new has occurred since we are between Culpepper and Fredericksburg. I hear no talk of a fight but I reckon they are fixing for another round somewhere. We don't meet very often here in Va but when we do we have bloody times. We are looking for E.M. to come to camp from the hospital today. Rick is well. I received a letter from John this morning. I was very glad to hear from all of the boys and to hear that W.R. Miner was not killed. We heard that he was killed dead and it looked like I never did hate to hear anything as bad in my life for we was always such cronies and had been together so much and to think he was killed but I hope he is not dead and will get away from the Yankees yet but they have got many of our friends in their hands and they are beginning to treat them very bad. I would not be surprised no time to hear of the Black Flag being raised on that account. There is some talk of it but I hope the people will use more humanity in this war than that. I am willing to defend our rights under a Civilized Banner but I am very much opposed to the Black Flag. But if the Yankees raises it first I will fight it but if our men raises it first then I am done. Give all the Vicksburg Boys my best repects. Tell them to keep in heart but I know it is bad to fight under officers without confidence.

I wish they had such officers as we have got. I think they would be more successful. General Lee has the confidence of our army. We don't doubt his loyalty. I would like to be at Sweetwater today. I guess you will have a fine time as it is Communion Day. I dreamt last night that I was there and Miss P.H. and her mother went home with me and when I got home you was mad with me I thought. It hurt my feelings to think I had worked so hard to get home and find you mad with me. But there is no chance for me to come home but I hope I will live to come sometimes. I want to see you all very bad. Give my love to all connections and friends. I have nothing else to write. Excuse this short letter for some of the boys wants my pen. Your loving son

    E.P.Landers to Susan Landers

To Miss H.C.Landers,

    A few lines to you Car. I am away off from camps about a half mile in an old outhouse upstairs by myself a studying about old times. I have saw more pleasure today than I have in a week for I am tired being with so many men. A person has to slip off if he ever gets to himself. I was glad to hear what you was all doing. Now you tell Sarah that I can't come before Sunday after my cider. I can almost taste it and them peaches in the old pasture. We have to pay 90cts a dozen for little hard things and can't get them at no price since we left Richmond. We have to spend a heap of money here. I give 1 dollar for my supper last night down on the river where we was at work. You requested me to send you a ring to remember me by. I will send it with pleasure if I can get one but us old dirty solgers don't have them in camp and I don't no whether I ever will see Richmond anymore or not. But I will send it the first chance. Give my respects to Miss P.H. and Matt and all the Sweetwater girls. Tell Mr. Mc that W.H. and Rob was well the other day. Tell little W.H. to sell mine and his lttle steers for he can't break them by himself. For the want of room I must close.

    E.P.Landers to H.C.Landers at home

Chancellorsville  April 1863
Dear H.C.

    I will write you a few lines but I have nothing gay nor flourishing to write. If I write any nuse it must be of a dismal character. You spoke of your fine meeting and pretty girls and of the beautiful rose vine. Car I would be glad if I could be there to enjoy the pleasant season of spring with my old friends but no such pleasure is for me. H.C. you wanted to know if I thought hard of you for spending my money. I don't call it my money after I send it home. I know that you will not spend it for what you don't need and what you really need that money is to get it with. I wish I was at home today so we could ride out on a visit. I would like to try Jane's springs again. I have not been on a horse since the evening before I left home. G. Davis said that they are a splendid hand at the plow. Be careful and don't let Kate run away. I wish I was there to take your place but I have something else to do. Give my love to friends.

       Your Brother E.P.Landers

Give my respects to Miss P.H. I wrote her last Sunday. Corporal N.A. Smith of our Co died April 30th with disease. Write soon and tell Liz and old T. to write. I hant got time or paper to write anymore. E.M. is tolerable well and is off on guard. He can't write today but he sends his entire respects to you all. He can't do much good here.
Our Great General Jackson is dead. Our own men shot him through a mistake on Saturday night but I just hope we can find another Jackson.

Weldon NC  March 23  1862

My Dear Mother,

       It has been a pleasure to me to write you a few lines in order to let you no my condition. I am tolerable well. This morning we're now on our way to Goldsborough, N.C. We left Suffolk yesterday and got to this place last night. We will stay hear tell this evening. We met Asa Wright hear last night. He was on his way to Suffolk. It is about 100 and 50 miles from Suffolk to the place that we are going. I have just read your letter and all was right in it. I was setting on the platform when I read it. I just turned round and is now riting on the place where I was setting. I'm glad of that money you sent but now I wish you had it back for I coulda dun without it for when I left Suffolk I got 4 dollars from A.W. and all of my mess is left in Suffolk but me. That is all in my tent. E.M. and Nute and Mayfield is down sick though I reckon that you have heard it for I wrot Unkle Eli a letter the other day. At that time we did not think that E.M. would live but when we left yesterday he was a great deal better. I think now by good attention he will soon get well. A.W. come from the hospital the next evening after I wrot Unkle Eli's letter. He is well and was left with E.M., Nute, and Mayfield. He's very bad off but is getting better. Well you heard a false tale about me starting to a battle and giving out. It is very true I did not get to the battle but I got as far as any of the rest did. We thought we was going in to a fight but the enemy did not come out to face the music. They say that they are fighting at the place we are going to. I wouldn't be surprised if we don't get to try it before many days and I won't care if we do but it makes me feel bad to think that out of my mess I am all that is able to carry arms but I will try to do my fighting and some for them too. I reckon we will be stationed at Kinston, N.C. but I don't know how long we will stay there. We will be 100 and 50 miles nearer home than we was at Yorktown. I haven't got time to write much. The train is nearly ready to start and I want to mail my letter before I start but if I had time I could write the bulliest letter ever you read from me for my heart is full. If I only could reveal it. I have got the worst cold I ever had and is now exposed and will be for several days. Sometimes we are gone from camp 2 or 3 days without a tent to lie in and very often in the snow or rain.. But I hope that the strong arm of protection will be with me through all of my trials. Give my love to all the friends. Capt and Luit Cain was left in Suffolk sick though I think they will be on in a few days. So without I could write a full letter I will close with my best wishes to you all and to our Country. The folks must not think hard of me for not riting for the truth is I don't have the chance to write since we left Yorktown. But my silence don't stop my respects to all my friends. I have writ this in great haste so goodby my dear old Mother.if I never see you again. I will write soon as we get stationed.

    E.P.Landers to Susan Landers

Camp Near Richmond  Aug 4th  1862

Dear Mother,

    As I have an opportunity to send by hand in great haste I will write you a few lines though you need not to expect much for it is nearly night and we have just come off drill. I am well this evening all but one of my jaws is swelled a little. I have nothing new to write at this time. I received your letter of the 16th of July an that is the only one I have received from you in a long time. I sent you a letter an 50 dollars by Mr. F.M.Beardin. Please let me no if you received it. Ther was 5 ten dollar bills. We are still at the same place one of the beautifulest camps and a plenty of the best kind of water but I am afraid that we will not stay hear long for they have commenced ther fighting again with the Yankee fleet on the James River. Last Thursday night they fired ther battery at the fleet for about 2 and a half hours supposing to do great damage. We have all enjoyed ourselfs finely since we have bin permitted to rest. We all appreciate this kind of living as hi as we used to at our homes. As it is most dark I must hasten through. Tell Moss Billy that R.N. is not well. He has bin reporting sick for about a week but he is not very bad off. W.P. Mason is complaining today. Liz, Pink wants you to send him a good pair of No. 9 shoes by the first one that passes. Ma I want you to send me a pair of No. 9's too if you please for I am nearly barefooted and shoes is so hi here. Well you must all do the best you can and I will do the same. I wish I had time to write a full letter but Mr. Ambrose will start soon in the morning and it is most dark. Please write soon and give me all the nuse. Give my entire respects to all the family an connections an inquiring friends. Mamma I think that I would sell what stock I could spare an rent out my land for you can't farm it yourself. So as it is getting dark with my best love an well wishes to you as a son. I will close. Excuse this short letter. I will write again soon so nothing more as I remain your affectionate son as ever.

      E.P. Landers to Susan Landers

Orange Co  Va  Aug 21st  1863

Dear Mother,

      I will send you a few lines in E.M.'s letter merely to let you no that I am well this evening hoping this will find you all well. I answered the last letter received from you stating the death of Brother N.B. and has bin patiently waiting to answer another. I think ther will be one for me when the mail comes in the morning. I hope so at least. I have nothing interesting to write at present. Ever thing is calm at present. No fighting going on about here now. I can't tell you anything about the position of the two Armies but our Army is at different points from Fredericksburg to Culpepper which is about 48 miles. I suppose that both armies is recruiting, fixing for another fight. We are 20 miles from Fredericksburg but I recon we will move camp tomorrow 15 miles from here in order to get forage for the horses. I am very willing for we have eat out this part of the country. General Lee has granted one man out of each regt a 24 day furlough. I guess that one of our Co will get one but it will be one that has never bin home. Sam Dyer will git one since one of his Co drawed for it and he got it. He is so proud he can't hardly behave himself. Mamma, if he comes I wish you would send me a pair of sox for I hant got nun and I don't like to do without and as you are making me a coat don't think that I am a great big man and make it too large. I am no heavier than I was when I left home. If you could git the pattern that Capt Cain's coat was cut by, you could exactly fit me for his coat fits me all round but his pattern may be over in Milton where you can't git it. I don't need no clothing at present. I could draw but the government clothes is so sorry and dear I had rather draw the money and send home than to draw the clothes. I am sorry to hear the dry weather has cut your crops short. I was in hopes the rain would continue and the crops be good. All military duty is suspended for today. The President has proclaimed this a day of fasting and prayer throughout the whole Confederacy but I think the most of the boys eats a heap and prays but little. But I believe that we will have to be more obedient than we are before we can expect to be delivered from this state of trouble. We will have to deny our strength and acknowledge the Almighty. A.W. I received your letter one night and never got to more than half read it for it was dark and John Wallis lost it. I hant got time to answer it for it is most night and we have to draw and cook a days rations and fix for moving. We will move in the morning at 5 o'clock. I wish that me and E.M. had holt of that basket of peaches you spoke of. We would save you of some trouble. I've not eaten one peach this year nor a ripe apple. Ever thing of that kind grows less plentiful in this army.

Mamma if your mare is fat she is worth more than 300 dollars the way ever thing is for it seems like that the Confederate money is not so current and I don't no what is the reason. Give my love to all the famly and connections and reserve a good portion for yourself. I will write you a letter when I hear from you. Write when you can and let me no wher Dan Miner is going. I wouldn't advise him to come to this Co. I have several good reasons for saying so, but nothing more.

     E.P.Landers to Susan Landers

Dear Mother,

     A few lines to you as I dont no when I will have the chance to write again. I am well today and I hope this will find you all well. You must read E.M.'s letter to git the nuse for I hant got time to write it to you both. I merely write this because I did not have time to send another one by Mr. Shamblee. I sent you 45 dollars by him. I told you I wanted you to pay Mrs. Reeder 13 dollars for me. I want you to pay her and git a receipt from her in my name. I said in my letter that ther was no prospect for a fight hear an the next morning the ball opened an we have had some of the beautifulest fighting that we ever have had. The greatest victory of all the War is this according to the number that was engaged. Cobb's Brigade has dun the work at last. It is the first time they ever had a showing an they have showed themselves. I was in the fight on Thursday but on Saturday I was detailed to cook. It is the first time I have ever bin out. I think we will try it again soon an I tell you I dread it. Of all the fights I've ever bin in I never had such feelings as I had on Thursday an I hope I never will have again. A good many of our Rgt was wounded that day and several killed. I want you to write soon. My Dear Mother if I never meet you again an should meet the dead fait of some of my friends I hope to meet you in a world of peace an pleasure. Ther is so many dangers stares me in the face I feel the need of a strong Protector. I sent you some needles by Mr. Shamblee. I merely sent them for compliments. Give my love to all the Family. Excuse these few lines. I will send it in E.M.'s letter so I will quit.

     E.P.Landers to Susan Landers

Portion of a letter which was probably written near Yorktown in 1863.

I written to Mr. Matthews concerning Jim. I waited on him 9 days after the fight till my hand got so I could use a gun. Then I went back to the Regt. Jim said that something plainly told him that if he went into a fight that he would get killed. There was several in our Regt that expressed their feelings before they went in and ever one got killed. Mamma I am glad you have paid all your debts for now is the time while you have got the money. I received that money you sent to me. I was not looking for it but it was very acceptable for I had to borrow some to help pay for my watch. Then I got 5 dollars from E.M. so me and him both was entirely without and had been for sometime so I will divide with him for he did with me as long as he had a cent. It will git us some paper stamps and envelops. Such things is very scarce and seem to grow less plentiful. Good paper is worth 5 dollars a quire. Everything is extremely high. Our wages will not clear our expenses.if we ever buy any little nicnacks especially them that chaws tobacco. My watch is a good doubled cased one. It is precisely like that one I kept of Motens awhile that he got from John Miner. You said that Kate was very unruly and that you was going to sell her and keep Jane. I expect if you had Jane broke that she would suit you the best for I think she is of a humble disposition. I am listening to hear of Kate's running away with Car. George Davis says she is in splendid order if you sell her be sure that you git the worth of her for she is worth a heap of money from 6 to 7 hundred dollars is my price on Jane. Now I say daily I feel in good heart that you will make plenty this year if no sickness occurs as I learn that wheat is promising. I want you to save all yours if there is any chance. You had better be looking out for a reaper before it gits ripe. I would pay a good price or git it saved. I wouldn't give a bushel of wheat a day if I could do any better. I don't know what the people will do about their tax. It will trouble some of them to pay it. This war has brought many troubles on us but let us support it to the last. Let none flinch nor falter but stand steadfast and honorably in defense of our rights and our country will be hard to redeem and let everyone bear a part. If you hear from N.B. let me know it. Write when you can and give me all the family nuse. Write how Mr. Matthews is getting along with his bottom land. Give him my entire love and respects. Give my love to all the connections and friends. Times is very different to what they was this time two weeks ago. The cannons were roaring, the balls flying, the wounded groaning and everything that was terror is now peace. While everything is quiet today may it remain so. Remember me your son. I close with love and gratitude towards you Dear Mother. Farewell.

E.P.Landers to Susan Landers

Portion of a letter written somewhere in Pennsylvania on the way to Gettysburg.

I sent a set of uniform buttons by George Walker to go on my coat. It was 16 big ones and 6 little ones. H.C. you seemed to fear that I would think bad of you for going to Newman. You wuz perfectly right in so doing. I am glad you went and as for getting your teeth plugged it was the best thing you could of done. I received your letter from Newman. I have saw a heap of pretty Yankey girls but somehow I can't help but hate them. H.C. give my respects to the Sweetwater girls. Tell them that I say the Yankey girls looks mighty well but I love them the best yet. It is most night and I have 2 days rations to cook so I had better close. Give my love to all the conncetions and inquiring friends. I may never live to get out of the U.S. again and if not remember where and how I left my life. I received a letter from E.M. today. He is at Lynchburg, Va He is tolerable well. Tell all my friends to not think hard if they don't hear from me soon for there is no chance for writing now. If I could see you all now I could tell you so many things that would interest you but I will close this short letter with my best love to you all. Remember me as your son and brother. I am well. Them risings is most all well now. Give my love to Mr. Mathews and Family. Don't be uneasy about me. Take care of yourselves. So nothing more this evening. It is Sunday. I could set here and write all evening but I must quit. Goodby to you all.

E.P.Landers your loving son and brother as ever

Portion of a letter

I hope you can make out by yourself for I don't know how you will save your wheat but if there is any chance I want you to save it all. Speak to Mr. Arnold and see if he won't cut it for the wheat or the money. If we ever draw I will send you money to pay him but I don't know when we will draw again. The Confederacy owes me 100 dollars besides my 50 dollars bounty that will be due me in August which I will send the most of to you if I ever get it. I want you to write soon and let me know what you have done with John and his steers and wagon and all the nuse that you think I want to hear and especially how your crop looks and how you all hold out to work and how you make out to plowing. If you can't send it in one letter send in two for I had rather read a letter from you now than anybody else. Give my best respects and well wishes to N.B. and Moten in your letter for I don't know where to write to them. Tell them to write me. Remember my respects to you all as your Best Friend and well wishes. But poor dependent people are deprived of the enjoyment of the pleasures at home that belongs to an independent people with the cussed invaders still trampling our homes and destroying our friends seeking every way to bring us to entire subjugation. It is enough to raise the passions of all persons that claims the title of independent. Mamma I understand by W.H. McDaniel that you have been bying more corn. I thought you had nearly enough to make out and I am afraid the rogues will steal it from you knowing that you are alone though it takes a heap to feed 2 horses. Well I have just taken a mess a boiled pies and read a letter from D.M. McDaniel and Mr. Garner. They was well. We have some of the hardest rains here that I ever saw. We just have to take it like young goslings but I reckon that the Yankeys has to take it some too. Give my best respects to all the connections and inquiring friends and tell little William Henry that he is my little boy. Pink has just come in to camp.

He is not clear of them pains yet though he is nearly well. All that was able to leave had to give up their beds to the wounded. There is thousands wounded from that battle. The boys is all around me so that I can't write as I would wish, but you must excuse me for you know that I would be glad to interest you all that I could and if I never see you no more keep this sorry letter in remembrance of me. H.C. I can hardly keep from crying of you and Add having to swing the plow but I can't help it. You must be careful with the horses and don't run too close nor too fur from the corn and write how your garden patch looks and if you can I want you to send me a wool hat and some thread and needles and a case to put them in for I have lost mine. Give my love to Sarah and little Pole and to Liz and the children. Mammy you need not send me any clothing for we have drawed a suit of clothes but if I send my money home in time you had better get your winter shoes before they get so high and if you can have me a good strong pair of firm shoes made for me for they are from 8 to 10 dollars a pair here. You had better get shet of all your cows and keep only one cow and calf. I want to know if you have ever got my overcoat and wool shirt or not. I sent them in Capt Reeder's trunk so as I have nothing to write I will bring my letter to a close with my best love to you all as an affectionate son and brother and if I never see you on earth let us endeavor to meet in a world where troubles and trials are all banished away. So remember my last respects is with you requesting you to write soon so nothing more.

Yours Respectfully,
E.P.Landers to Susan Landers